# SEND IN THE CONGREGATION
## Stories from the Foo Fighters Fans

Rachael Gilliver

**ISBN:** 978-1-980337-69-0

Rachael Gilliver and Roswell Publishing are not associated with with Foo Fighters or their management.

Cover photograph © Sarah Turrel (Instagram: @sarah.turrell)
Cover design Lucy Kong (lucykongcreative.com)

For the Gilliver clan,
Because the music really does sound better with you!

# CONTENTS

Foo Fighters:

1. An unidentified flying object which was often described as a bright ball of light or fire. Originally seen by fighter pilots during World War II. The objects' name was generally considered to be a reference to the comic strip Smokey Stover as well as a play on the French word for fire.

2. American rock band formed and fronted by Dave Grohl. Other members include Taylor Hawkins, Nate Mendel, Chris Shiflett, Pat Smear, and Rami Jaffee. The band has been together for over twenty years, won numerous awards, and sold over forty million albums worldwide.

Dear Dave, Taylor, Chris, Nate, Pat, and Rami,

What would I say if you were sitting beside me? Would I thank you for your music or all the times that you've made me laugh? Or would I remember the times that I've seen the weight of the world resting on your shoulders and reach out to give you a hug? Truth be told, I'm not sure what I'd say to you.

While I may not know what to say, the people within the pages of this book certainly do. Their stories have lead them to one thing; that you, and your music, have done something positive in their lives. Whether it's friendships, a lifeline in life's darkest moments, learning to live through your lyrics, or the global community that surrounds the band, their words run like a river around you. And that is one of the primary reasons that I wrote this book. I was adopted in to the fan groups even though I had little to no interest in your music. It wasn't my thing and, to me, foo fighters is a term that's used in another part of my life (I spend *a lot* of time watching the skies!). I just didn't *get* your music; for me it was pop-rock chart music that would be forgotten as soon as an album cycle was over. But the wonderful people that I'd met had piqued my curiosity. I wanted to know

9

*why* people were willing to go to a stadium and stand in a crowd with 80,000 other people. I wanted to know *why* they returned to your albums time and again. I wanted to know *why* they talked about you as though you were family. I wanted to know *why* they'd welcomed someone like myself as though *I* was long lost family. So I asked them one simple question: Why do you love this band as much as you do?

I'm sure that, like many of us, you have had times when life is pulling you down, the weight resting on your back like a boulder. This book is for those moments. It's a reminder of all that you've done and all that you'll leave behind. You've touched the lives of millions of people and a few of them chose to put their stories down for the world, and for you, to read. They're tales of pain, despair, and hurt that were morphed into love, excitement, and happiness because of you.

*Because of you.*

Because of you, and all that you have done, people have found a reason to keep on going. They've found a reason to keep on living and to keep on giving. They've found a reason to get up in the morning. They've found a reason to love and to laugh. There may be times when you think that you're little more than a rock and roll band. But, to many people, you're far more than that.

You're not just a band. You're a group of human beings who wear their hearts on their sleeves. You share your passion with those who come to your shows and who listen to your albums. You've made them smile every day and never once have you broken their hearts or told them that they're not worth your time. You've never left them and have always included them in all that you do. For the fans, you're like that neighbour who invites them to sit on the porch and shoot the breeze. For them, you will always be far more than "just a band".

In a world that feels as though it's beyond redemption, you've given people something positive to hang on to. You music, your lyrics, and everything that you say and do restores the hope that people were rapidly losing. Your openness and willingness to embrace others has formed bridges across cultural divides. Your humbleness inspires other people to do the same. You, and the rest of the band, are loved beyond measure. Loved by people who, if you ever have an hour of need, will be there to support you just as you've done for them.

What would I say to you? Thank you for bringing love, laughter, and music into a world that can feel as though it's out to get us. Thank you for reminding us that there is always light at the end of the tunnel, no matter how hard life can become. Most of all, thank you, to you and everyone who surrounds you, for just being yourselves. I'd also give you that hug because sometimes it's the simplest of gestures that can say the most.

This is your legacy. Enjoy it!

Love and inky trails,
Rae

# INTRODUCTION

Communities thrive wherever there are people. In the nooks and crannies of society you'll find gatherings dedicated to everything from knitting and crochet to popsicle model-making and the intricacies of sheds. Often these groups are formed from people in the locality of where we live and these impromptu bands of people are where friendships are formed and nurtured, giving us the human interaction that is so essential to our psychology.

But what if we can't find a local group that we fit in with? What if your primary interests aren't conducive to what is on offer and there is little incentive to set up such a group?

Over the past decade online communities have grown at an astonishing rate and have come to exist not just in cyberspace but also in real life. The internet has become a place where, with the simple click of a button, a space can be created and people who you have no other connection to other than a shared interest can be invited. Those strangers become friends and, over time, those friends become family. Much is often made of the dangers of the internet and how it is negatively impacting our lives. Yet, in the case of many people, the opposite is true. Unable to find people with common interests in their local area, they have turned to the internet in order to feed that most basic desire of feeling needed and wanted.

Online they can let their personalities shine and grow and integrate themselves with people who share similar interests.

Human interaction is vital to our health and well-being. At our core, we are herd animals who feel safer when we are around others. Even if we identify as introverted there's still a need to have companionship. There's a need to have discussions, to talk through issues, and to know that we are loved and cared for. For some people this isn't provided by those in their immediate vicinity such as family or local friends. Finding an online community becomes important in their lives so that they can feel the comfort of knowing that there are people like themselves out there. Prolonged isolation, as has been seen in a variety of studies, can change the way that a person thinks or acts. Being with others, sometimes just in a work or retail environment, can be beneficial to their health and has been proven to lower anxiety and depression.

Being a part of a community, whether in the physical or online worlds, is just one piece of what makes us human. Knowing that there is someone next door, at the end of the phone, or reading our email can gives us the sense of safety that so many of us crave. We live in a world that feels so uncertain and many people are finding that their fears are coming to the surface. Often these fears have nowhere to go except back down into their being. Being able to let go of the festering negativity can be a release valve and help to bring a person in to a more stable frame of mind. On the flip side, having a place to celebrate the highs of life can bring the validation and happiness that we need as human beings.

Having somewhere to talk about our feelings is especially important in an age that's feeling more and more fragmented. While technology has the ability to bring us together it can also push us apart. Everyone and anything is available at the touch of a button yet this instantaneous access to global knowledge pushes some to feel isolated and alone. Dating seems to have become that little bit harder while getting tickets to popular shows and events has turned in to a monumental climb to the top of a technological mountain. Despite having the world at our fingertips, life seems a little harder than it was ten or twenty years ago with the innocence of those decades washed away by the glow of a computer screen.

The importance of having a solid community has become even more vital in these computerised days. We desire interaction with others and a need to know that we're not alone. When life feels as though it is moving too fast, being able to talk to someone close is a rare moment to stop and live life in the present. We're not thinking about what needs to happen in the next hour. Instead, we've paused our life and we're spending time with those we love. Sometimes that may be a meeting that happens in person or it may be an exchange of messages via social media. To feel that connection, no matter what form it comes in, is important to in an age where life feels as though it's becoming more automated.

Building sustainable communities online is as important as ones that are created in the real world. People need places to interact in ways that technology can't. At the moment computers can't replicate human emotion in a way that a person can. Communities that are given an opportunity to thrive and who welcome in all walks of life are the ones that are most likely to succeed.

So how do music fans fit in to all of this?

This book takes a look at the ever growing and ever changing community that surrounds fans of American rock band Foo Fighters. Going by the collective name of "Foo Family" their space is one of friendship and generosity, one that welcomes any stranger who happens to wander off the beaten path and in to their embrace. Rather than a single online meeting place, the Foo Family are more of a digital city that encompasses social media, forums, websites, and chat groups. Their presence criss-crosses multiple plains and overspills in to real life with meet ups at concerts, hotels, and people's homes. Like a support group for those who follow one of America's biggest rock bands, they connect new members to others living in their local area, giving them someone that they can connect to and, at some point, hopefully meet. I have several such people on speed dial, some living as close as

Birmingham while some are as far flung as America and Australia.

As with real life, the Foo Family moves in cycles. People come and go and some return. Arguments happen but so do make-ups. Life, death, births, and marriages are all recorded upon the group's various pages as they capture the ups and downs of life.

Among the various highways and byways of this mostly cyber family people have found a place to call home. Where blood relationships fail so those friendships, built from meetings at shows and online, become the surrogate family that many have been looking for. There, in the sometimes secret groups of social media, they're allowed a platform to vent their darkest fears and biggest dreams in relative safety. Somewhere, someone will always be online to catch you if you fall.

And fall they do as this is a band who, through their music, have saved lives. People who have been on the brink of suicide have found solace in the sometimes lullaby quality of Foo Fighters songs. Wrapped in the Midwestern lilt of Dave Grohl's voice they can drift away on an ocean of chords as they find the strength to heal and move on with life. In turn, their stories of survival become an inspiration to those who may have found themselves in a bottomless pit of family problems or ill health.

But what makes a music fan? Is it someone who spends thousands of pounds a year on their favourite band and goes to see twenty shows? Or is it someone who never sees a live show yet quietly appreciates an artist? Is it someone who is actively involved in a band's fan groups? Or someone who sits somewhere in the middle, never really participating but wanting to be a part of it all the same?

Circumstances dictate a lot of what a person can do from resources to cash flow to whether they feel comfortable in a crowd. Their favourite musicians may never pass through their town and their situation in life may dictate whether they can travel or not. Day to day matters such a childcare, health issues, transport, and distance are all issues that have to be factored in to attending a live show, issues that hold so many people back from being what they may see as a "true fan". While we have online shopping, some retailers may not deliver to certain locations or shipping costs may make buying records and merchandise cost-prohibitive. On the flip side, services like Spotify make it easier for the resource strapped fan to access new releases while social media allows them to stay in the loop for news and events.

For many fans money is a big issue especially when it comes to concert tickets. Live concerts are an experience in themselves, especially for dedicated followers of a band. Not only is it a chance to see their favourite artists perform but it's also an opportunity to meet up with people who they may only have spoken to online. Live shows are a chance to build friendships that will last through any hardship. Yet with ticket prices rising faster than wages going to see a band can be a financial strain that has to be carefully budgeted for. Taking in to account current unstable employment environments and the transient nature of the population you begin to see the divide between the "have's" and the "have not's" of music fans. Many fans will budget for tours by taking on extra jobs, working more hours, or selling prized possessions in order to purchase tickets. Those on fixed incomes have it the hardest and, while writing this book, I saw instances of people buying tickets only to have to sell them at the last moment due to financial constraints. Some fan groups account for this and have developed pools of resources that support those who may otherwise struggle. These groups may offer help with accommodation, transport, or collecting money to purchase spare tickets that are then passed on to those who wouldn't otherwise be able to afford them.

While there are always shows to go to, many fans have, at some point, found themselves staring down the barrel of a proverbial gun. Ticket touting is a big business, one which, in the UK alone, nets around £2,000,000,000 in revenue. Despite outcries from the music going public and MPs, the secondary ticket market is one which largely goes ignored by those higher up the governmental chain. In 2014 the UK Foo Family took action in the shape of a crowdfunded Foo Fighters show with the hopes of showing the world that concert ticketing could be done differently. While the show never happened, the group easily met their £150,000 target and helped to bring the issue of the secondary ticket market to a global audience. Thanks to campaigns such as this one, bands are beginning to listen and are bringing in practices to make it easier for everyone to attend their shows rather than just those who can afford to pay the inflated prices of the touts. Ticketing agencies such as TicketMaster have been targeted for unfair practices and, in August 2017, the London offices of ticket touts Viagogo and StubHub were raided in an ongoing investigation into breaches of consumer law. Slowly but surely, the power is being put back into the hands of passionate fans and once more giving them the opportunity to experience their favourite artists live. Some would like to believe that these little forward steps are a response to their ongoing campaigns against unfair ticketing practices. And maybe, just maybe, they are.

Amazing things happen when fans get together. There was the previously mentioned No More Touts concert from the UK. In 2015, one thousand people in Italy played Foo Fighters *Learn To Fly* in an attempt to get the band to play in their area. It worked and, on November 3rd 2015, Foo Fighters played in Cesena, Italy. After waiting more the sixteen years for the band to return and not wanting to wait any longer, fans in Richmond, Virginia crowdfunded a show. The band responded by playing the show in September 2014.

When Laura Plane passed away from cancer, her husband, Jon, attempted to get the band to dedicate *Everlong* at their Glastonbury headlining set. His attempts paid off and, in June 2017, the song was played in her memory.

The fan groups that I've become a part of both in real life and online are a mix of people from all walks of life. All of them have giving hearts no matter where they're from, nor what their income is. Every year they raise money for a nominated charity and have donated tens of thousands of pounds to causes close to their hearts. However, the fan groups aren't without their dark moments. During the course of this book, I witnessed Foo Fighters fans work through scams as unscrupulous people played on the generous nature of the groups in order to solicit funds for their own ends. To see their trust broken was painful and heartbreaking. For a while the groups were fragmented with people coming and going as they tried to gather their thoughts and emotions before they regrouped and continued with their charitable works.

Community is a strange word to attribute to an online collective. But it fits, far more than we give it credit for. These are people who've built an online home for themselves, a place where they can go and rest, play, and talk. Much like a community that is built of bricks and mortar, they gather in the place where they accepted and where their views are respected. A community isn't a physical place as much as it's a gathering of people who accept and love one another for what they are.

While putting *Send in the* Congregation together, I decided that one of the best ways to portray the Foo community was by keeping each person's voice as intact as possible. Every chapter is a direct transcription of each person's interview and has only been lightly edited in order to preserve their unique voice and perspective.

# Julia
## Bath, UK

Kerrang TV, believe it or not, was the first place that I saw the Foos. I've been a fan for about seventeen years. I was a bit of a late starter compared to some. I have no idea what the first song I heard was, probably because it was on the television.

I know how my obsession with them started and it was through Dave playing with Queens of the Stone Age. When I saw Dave drumming with them on the video for *No-one Knows* I was like "Who is that guy? Because he's super-fit and look at him drumming." And that's how I got in to the Foo Fighters.

What does the band mean to me? In one word: Everything. Because they've carried me through everything. All the bad times, all life's ups and downs, and they've brought me through really horrible times when I was literally suicidal and had nobody else to turn to or talk to. I don't have family around me and so I felt really alone. They bought me through all of that and obviously, when I got out the other side of that, they bought me to my soul mate because I met Lee through their music. And all of my closest friends, who I obviously call family, the Foos bought me all of that as well. There literally isn't an aspect of my life that they haven't been really instrumental in. You can't overstate it when I say that my whole, entire life is literally interwoven with them.

I've seen them live and, while I haven't counted for a while now, but it's probably about sixteen times. I saw them five or six times in 2015 and again when they played the Cheese and Grain in Frome.

The Cheese and Grain? Yeah, that was a shocker. We weren't expecting that, were we?! All of a sudden Foo Fighters are like, "Yeah, we're just coming to England.". I was at the tattoo shop getting tattooed and scrolling through my phone, like you do, and I saw that people were getting tickets from the Foo Fighters through the post. Obviously no one had signed up for anything and no one could have applied for anything because we didn't know what the Hell it was. None of us had any idea what was going on.

The first I knew about it was when Rachel got hers. She lives about two streets away from me. I thought that if Rachel had tickets then there's hope for me. Obviously nobody knew what they were but I was thinking that they had to be for some kind of show. Even though they were so-called boarding passes, they were obviously tickets for a show of some sort. But there was so much speculation and with it saying "Obelisk Airlines" we guessed that that was to do with the Pyramid Stage and therefore Glastonbury. Which we kind of already knew that they were going to be playing anyway. So we had no idea because we didn't have tickets for Glastonbury. I phoned my twelve year old daughter and asked her if there was any post. No, no post. I said that if any post came that she was to let me know. So I sat there all day in the tattoo shop and there was nothing. No post. Nothing. Got home that night and obviously nothing had happened so I was a bit gutted. And we'd seen on Twitter and a couple of other places that other people had got tickets. But they all seemed to be in the Bath area, which was really, really weird because Foo Fighters aren't just going to rock up to Bath and play because that just would be too odd.

The next day I was working, which was a Sunday, and I was working in two different places, one place in the morning and one in the afternoon. And I had about half an hour to come home and get changed and maybe eat something. I came home and there was a card on the door mat, one of the "Sorry We Missed You" cards from Royal Mail. And I was like, "Shit! This could be the tickets!". I'm sure I hadn't ordered anything and I was racking my brains, trying to work out if I'd bought anything and forgotten about it. So I was trying not to get overexcited in case I got down to the Post Office and found out that it was just something that I'd ordered off of eBay. I phoned Lee up, because he was at work, and asked him if I'd ordered anything. He said that he was fairly sure that I hadn't. But it was Sunday so I couldn't go to the Post Office and pick them up. Lee reminded me that they're open on a Sunday morning but I said that you have to wait until the day after to pick anything up because the card had only just arrived. So I hung up and looked at the card and, of course, they'd tried to deliver the day before. They'd obviously knocked on the door on the Saturday and no one had answered and we'd all come home that night and not seen the card that had been pushed through the door.

It suddenly dawned on me that, as it's the day after they'd tried to deliver them, I could go and get them now. So I jumped in the car and everyone in Bath was suddenly out in their car on a Sunday and I was like, "Where are you people going?! It's Sunday!". It was the craziest thing you've ever seen! I was even aware of how crazy I looked while I was doing it! I was driving like a bat out of Hell. So I got there and obviously it was an A4 envelope just the same as everyone else's had come in. I took it outside and, before I opened it, I phoned Lee and I was opening the envelope just as he answered the phone. He was like, "Well?" and just as he said that, I opened the envelope and said, "Yeah! It is! It's our tickets!". We still don't what they were for; we were just glad that we had some! Because obviously they had the departure airport was LAX and the arrival was CAG. Obviously I'd been mulling it over and as I was getting ready for bed, I said, "Cheese and Grain!". Then I was like, "No, they're not going to play at the Cheese and Grain.". Because obviously it's small and it's in the middle of nowhere. And who the Hell goes to Frome?!

On the Tuesday afternoon, Lee phoned the Cheese and Grain and got the box office. He asked, "So, can you tell me when Foo Fighters are playing, please, because I need to get the day off work?". And the guy in the box office was like, "What? I don't know what you're talking about. I haven't heard anything about that.". Lee was looking at me and going, "He's lying. He's lying.". He could tell that the guy was lying. So we were pretty confident that we'd sussed out where they were playing. But we still didn't know why or know anything else about it.

We had to check-in online and when we checked in we obviously had to put the ticket number in. And when we checked in, it said, "Congratulations! Your adventure begins on Thursday" and to wait for an email on the Thursday night.

But we had tickets for another gig on the Thursday. So we were in Bristol, waiting, and we'd gone to the pub for something to eat before the gig. And it was about 5.55pm when the email came through and we found out what it was. Obviously we were mega excited. So we gave our tickets to Me First and the Gimme Gimmes to the barman and went home! We didn't even go to the gig we were supposed to go to! We were like, "Fuck it! Give them to the barman and he can give them to someone.". We were too excited to even do anything else other than go home!

The trouble was that we were both supposed to be working on the Friday. Lee's boss is great and he just said to his boss, "Look, I really need Friday off. Can I swap and work Sunday instead?". It's a bit different for me because I'm a carer and I care one to one so if I'm not there there's nobody there to look after the person that I should be with. The lady I was looking after is a new client that I was working with and I was really the only one who was trained to work with her. We'd had one other carer come in and do a couple of shadow shifts and that was it. So I thought that I was screwed. What I was doing with that client was four hours in the morning and four hours in the afternoon. I said that I'd work in the morning and stay an hour later so that they wouldn't be on their own. So I managed to get the new person to cover for me in the afternoon. And then I had to phone my boss and tell her. To be fair, I was expecting her to hit the roof because I'd arranged it all behind her back! I'd called the other carer and spoken to my client and said, "I really need to do this as it's a once in a lifetime opportunity.". Thankfully, everyone was fine about it.

Once I'd spoken to my boss, and she was okay with it, I got really tearful at work. The relief of being able to go, and I hadn't realised before how worried I was that my boss was going to kick off and something was going to happen to prevent me from going, I got quite emotional! We knew that, with the Cheese and Grain being such a small venue, that it was going to be really special and we knew that we had to get there.

So I worked in the morning and stayed an extra

hour with my client. Lee drew the short straw and caught the bus to the Cheese and Grain in the morning so that he'd be first in line. He was wrapped up in a sleeping bag because it was so cold. While he was there, he was interviewed on the news about why he was standing in line!

I picked up Rachel, who lives two streets away and is in a wheelchair. We got down there at about 2pm to keep Lee company. We saw all the cars pulling up and Pat came and spent time with us. He signed autographs and took photos with everyone who wanted them. When they opened the doors, Lee made a run for the rail and was in tears because he was right in front of Dave's mic. They'd put Rachel over to one side by the fire door and, before the show, we could see her waving at us. She ended up right behind us on the second row. The people around her were great and formed a human shield around her so that she didn't get any shit from anyone.

We were only in there for about an hour before the band came on. They made the announcement that they'd come over to sign the contracts for Glastonbury. The show was incredible. Like, how many times are the Foo Fighters going to personally invite you to one of their shows? It was great to see their energy and the little parts where they messed up. Don't get me wrong; a huge, polished show is great. But you also want to see these guys as human, too, and those little mess ups in songs, or jam sessions, or Dave playing reggae is what it's all about.

They played both of Lee's requests (*Wattershed* and *For All The Cows*) but Dave wouldn't play mine (*Stacked Actors*) because it's been ten years since they last played it. I think the last time that I saw them play *Stacked Actors* live was at Reading in 2008 but it's been dropped from the set list since then. Even when I see it on a video, like of a show in another country, I still get emotional because it's one of my favourite songs.

During the show, Dave was saying how freaky it was to see everyone on the front row with tattoos of his face on them [Dave spoke directly to Julia during the show and mentioned that he was going to get a photo of them together and have it tattooed on himself.]. Because we were on the front row, we were able to get stuff from the stage after the show had finished; setlists, guitar picks, things like that.

After the show we went outside to wait for the band. There were quite a few people waiting and security kept telling us that the band had already left. That was entirely possible because we'd had a quick drink at the bar and bought a load of merch before going outside. Some of the people left until there was only about twenty five of us. Security were really adamant that the band had gone but we decided to wait it out. About ten minutes after that, Dave came out with Pat. Lee pretty much collapsed in to Dave's arms and thanked him for playing *Wattershed*. It was a proper bromance moment! I told him [Dave] that the music had saved my life and he said, "I'm glad that you're still here.", which he didn't have to say.

He put his arms around both of us for a photo. We've made up a frame with all the stuff from the Frome show; the setlists we got, our wristbands and tickets. We've had the photo of the three of us (Julia, Dave, and Lee) blown up on to a canvas for our wall. It's about a metre wide!

What's the most special story I have relating to them? I met Lee. Obviously I didn't meet him because of the Foo Fighters. I met him because of the *Rage Against The Machine Christmas Number 1* campaign so, again, that's another social media story right there. But when that group was kind of grinding to a halt because Christmas had come and gone and people were going their own separate ways, Lee had posted in there that he'd got his tickets for Foo Fighters and I was like, "Oh, another Foo Fighters fan.". I'd already clocked him and we were quite chatty in that group anyway. But he posted in that group that he'd got his tickets for Milton Keynes and I was like, "Awesome". I added him to the Foo Family so that I wouldn't lose contact with him when we all disbanded from the Rage group. I was with someone at the time so that was as far as that went with Lee. But when we split up, Lee was the guy that I instantly thought of. I wasn't interested in having another relationship. I wanted to be single because I felt like I'd had such a nightmare in the past few years and I was like, "That's enough of that.". I wanted to be single and do my own thing and not have to cook tea for someone every night was going to be really nice! Just totally get out of the routine and rut that I'd been in for so long. But within ten days of us splitting up it just happened to be a Foo Family meet and the first one that Lee was going to. It was the first time that I'd met him face to face and, as they say, the rest is history.

Then there was our wedding because that was obviously all Foo-ish. The guys were all wearing Foo Fighters shirts under their suit jackets and we had Foo Fighters songs played at the wedding. We were going to go for a white limo but we couldn't fit eighteen people in a limo. So we had to have a white stretch Hummer instead and there were eighteen of us hanging out of it with "White Limo" playing at a million decibels. And obviously, last year [2015], we went to America because it was the band's 20th anniversary gig and it just happened to be my fortieth birthday. I was like, "Right, this year I'm going to spend loads and loads of money on having fun.". Because, when you have kids, everything goes to them. So I said, "I'm going to see them in America. I'm going to see them in Italy, and I'm going to see them at every single show that they play in the UK.". So I did that last year. Although, obviously, Dave breaking his leg fucked up a lot of my plans but we still got to see them play twice in America which was amazing. I think 2015 was about £10,000 worth of Foo Fighters.

I'm going to be paying for it for the next two years but it was worth it. Any time they do anything, I'm like, "Take my money!".

I think I've probably got one of the biggest [merchandise] collections that there is. I've got posters everywhere, photographs, drumsticks, plectrums. Guitars everywhere. I've got a replica DG335. We've got a Dan Armstrong Plexi that Dave played in one of the videos. We've got Foo Fighters lyrics painted on the stairs. Some of the people in the group call it the "Fooseum" because it is all over the walls in my house. I've got over 250 Foo Fighter tshirts now and over 200 magazines with Foo Fighters on the front cover. I'm like a thirteen year old who didn't get any older! You know, when you were thirteen and you had posters? That's me except that I'm nearly 41! We've got some stuff that's quite special to us and very unusual. We've got a drumhead that was signed by the whole band that was donated when we were raising the money for Kerry to go over to America. They donated that for auction but we raised so much money in the end that we decided to give it to Kerry as a gift rather than sell it. When we were getting married, Kerry was coming to the wedding and we asked if we could borrow the drumhead to use as the ring cushion. So we used the signed drumhead to put our wedding rings on. When she brought it to the wedding, she said, "I want you to keep it. It's your wedding present. I don't want it back.". So that's special because it came directly from them [the band] and because it was an amazing gift from a friend. I think the stuff that I like the most is the drumsticks and plectrums that I've caught myself at shows. When they did the three shows in 2014 as The Holy Shits, I don't know how I managed to get a ticket to each one of those. I don't know anyone else who managed to go to all three; there must be people out there who did but I haven't met them yet. So to have those three wristbands framed, that's quite special as well. It's the stuff that you can't buy that's the special things. It's the stuff that someone's given you or you've caught from a show. It's quite personal. Even when I was at the show, Taylor's drum tech, he's a really friendly guy, came out and he said that he'd noticed me there the day before. He came out either on the second or third night and he had a handful of plectrums. He gave me this massive handful of plectrums and I said, "Mate, I don't want one because I've one of each. Why don't you give them to these other guys who don't have one?". And he said, "No, I want you to have one.". So I said, "Why do I need a big bowlful of plectrums when there's guys here, who are just as big fans as I am, who don't have one?". I did say to him that if he really wanted to help me out that I had a friend back home who really wanted a drumstick and, bless him, he came back after the show and gave me one of Taylor's drumsticks. So all of this stuff is up on the walls of my house and every six months or so we'll have a rejig. Because we can't get it all up now so we have to move it around!

Personally, I think now they're now a classic rock band because they've been around for so long and that's kind of their sound. Just the best band in the world, really!

If I had to give someone one of the band's songs then I'd play them my favourite one because, well, it's my favourite and also because it's quite middle of the road. You wouldn't go directly to *White Limo* because that's a little bit too hectic for most people's tastes. So it would be *Times Like These*, which is my favourite.

My husband, thankfully, is cut from the same cloth so doesn't mind me being a fan. My brother just rolls his eyes! I've just surrounded myself with people who I've managed to brainwash sufficiently in to thinking being such a big fan is normal!

The Foo Family is what this band are going to leave behind. Obviously they're going to have the discography and that's never going to go anywhere. People are always going to recognise that the band have been consistent and hard working because they're always doing something. But, for me, it's going to be the Foo Family because there's about 15,000 of us in that one group and obviously there's hundreds of thousands of massive Foo Fighters fans around the world. It's not just a Facebook group. It doesn't just sit there and do nothing. It's a very big group of people that do stuff for each other all the time. People are always offering support to each other, helping each other out, and socialising with each other. You can't underestimate what that can do for a human who is on their own and to be able to feel connected to the world and to other people. It's a massive thing. I know some people say that it's "just the music" and "just the band", but it's really not. You could speak to a hundred thousand Foo Fighters fans and they'd talk about the music being the legacy. But, for me, it's about how the music has affected all those people. We fundraise to take people to gigs or to do something with them or to help them out when they've needed it. It's a massive thing and you don't find that in every day life. You don't get groups of people throwing money at someone because they're in the shit. It just doesn't happen. But it does in the Foo Family and I think it makes a massive difference. Because it just goes to show that when they're not touring, the group's not silent and it's not that there isn't anything going on. We're still socialising and still doing our thing. People don't go away just because the Foos aren't touring or because they didn't just bring out an album.

When we started the group, we were ignorant to the fact that there's a lot of Foo Fighters fans who call themselves "Foo Family" because it was happening on different platforms that we weren't on. Obviously, Kelly set the group up. I think it was originally called "I'm Going to See the Foo Fighters at Milton Keynes

Bowl 2011". It was set up for the people that were going to those shows and was for them to organise where they were going to camp and meet. But she left the group set to open, not realising that any Tom, Dick, or Harry who had tickets to go and see Foo Fighters in Milton Keynes could go and join this group. By the time the gig came along, there was probably a few dozen of us in there that had been chatting amongst ourselves for months. Then after the gig happened, people had become really good friends and we didn't want to shut the group down. So we renamed it "Foo Family" because, obviously, we're like family. Originally, it was just people from the gig who joined and they were mostly English. But as time went by, anyone from around the world who were Foo family, were joining and it grew from there.

# Ollie
## Ilkley, UK
### (Roadie with UK Foo Fighters)

I first discovered the band, and this is going to show my young age here, in probably 2006 just before *Echoes, Patience, Silence, and Grace* came out. My step-dad went to see the Foos at Wembley for the 2008 gig and he bought me back a Foos t-shirt. I was kind of familiar with them; you listen to the radio and *The Pretender* is on and I'd heard *Everlong* when I was 5 or 6 unknowing that it would change my life. So he bought me that t-shirt back. Then, of course, along with that I then wanted to buy the album. So I bought *Echoes, Patience, Silence, and Grace*, and pretty much the rest is history!

I'm going to say that the first song that I heard was *Learn to Fly* just because I always used to watch music TV when I was a kid and *Learn to Fly*, because of the video, was always on.

I'm quite fortunate in a way to have quite a unique connection with the band because of the UK Foos stuff. But even before I got involved with that, which was about five years ago, my love for the band basically went in to a full blown obsession straight away. Like many people, you hear an album, then you want to go and see a show, and then you want to see more shows, and then you want to go and buy all the albums that you missed out on because you're late to the party. So I bought the first Foo Fighters album after I bought *Wasting Light*. I guess the band have just become a way of life. I'd say that me and Jay [UK Foo Fighters front man] talk about the band pretty much every day in some format, whether it's something to do with a show of ours or something that the Foos have done, or how we're going to market the next tour. Everything kind of just boils down to them. Even when I listen to new bands it always comes back to the Foos in some way. But that's the beauty of it is that we've got twenty-two years worth of material and everything in between; side projects and EP's etc. Taylor's bought out three or four albums by himself, which I've then bought and loved and which I probably would never have heard of if I hadn't listened to the Foos in the first place. Taylor's a massive influence on me as a drummer. All my style is basically him. I'm aware of how much the band have shaped my life but I don't think that I'm aware of the scale just because everything, musically, is massively influenced by them.

How did I get involved with the UK Foos? Alex [UK Foo Fighters drummer] and I have played cricket together for quite a long time and we both live in the same town. He invited me to a local show where they were supporting Dr Feelgood, just a really low key kind of show. I was aware of the band's existence so I went and watched the show. I thought it was pretty good. Then, in 2013 on the first O2 Academy tour, he said, "Well, why don't you come and take a few pictures?". At that point, it was one instrument each, small amps, and small, intricate details that we'd copied from the Foos that perhaps nobody was really that aware of. Since I've been involved the band's just kind of snowballed in to this monster of amps, guitars, how we dress, the stage set up etc. Everything is absolutely identical to the Foos.

I've seen them at Leeds Festival, Invictus Games, Manchester, Milton Keynes, and I also want to say T in the Park. This is when you realise that your addiction is real!

Without going in to the lovely dovey, "Dave Grohl, I want your babies", type thing, we met Rami last year. He was playing with a guy called Johnny Kaplan on Brick Lane in London. There was probably twenty people at the show. It was a beautiful day, we were in the middle of London, it was like thirty degrees. Jay, Alex, and I all went down, kind of not really knowing what the environment was going to be like. We just knew that Rami was playing with this guy and that we might be able to have a quick chat with him. We arrived at the venue, walked in, and Rami was just sound-checking. The first thing he [Rami] said was, "Hey Jay, how's it going?". We took Nick [Keys for UK Foo Fighters] with us as well just so that Nick could meet his American alter ego. Basically it then ended up, for the rest of the night, for probably four or five hours with us just hanging out with him. He told us stuff about the recording of *Saint Cecilia* because it was fresh at that time and had only been out for a few months. He told me how the ideas came about and where they were and what they were doing when they decided to record it and how Dave had this complete shock reaction of, "Oh my God, I'm bored. Why don't we make an album?". We thought that we might get a quick five minute chat with him. But we sat on this sofa, watching him play. They played some Stones songs and this kind of laid back country music. And then I stood on stage and watched him play. He was just so relaxed with all of us. But we literally spent from four in the afternoon to the early hours of the morning with him.

I counted them the other day, basically because I had to iron half of them, that I had ninety-seven or ninety-eight Foo Fighters or Foo Fighters related t-shirts. But I'm including Them Crooked Vultures and Taylor's ones in that count. We have a thing where whenever Dave or Taylor wears anything we will get on Google and try to find it. I've got quite a few weird t-shirts that people might not know that Taylor wore once in 2004. But that's about the authenticity of the band is that when Dave wears a new t-shirt, we'll find it and next gig Jay'll be wearing it.

I think the Foos are just going to be "that band". Everyone has that one band that they always come back to. Even if the band went away or even if I went off them, which obviously wouldn't happen but even if it did, I know that I'd come back to them. They really are "that band" and that, no matter what they release, you always try and find the good parts.

They're not really rock. It's more like they're forged their own genre a bit. They're kind of like soft rock but then some of the riffs, like *All My Life*, sound like they belong on a Disturbed or Metallica album. So they're kind of like alternative rock, I'd say. They're so talented and they've got such a varied genre that if there's one song you don't like it's almost guaranteed that there's another song on the same album that you do like. Recently, at rehearsal, we played *In The Clear* again. Which, obviously, we had the whole music video thing that went around that [In 2015, the UK Foo Fighters recorded a version of "In The Clear" and released it as a charity single. The single, and subsequent video, can be found online.]. On the day of the video I think that we probably played it about eighty times and then had a show the same night where we played it again then. Everyone got sick of it so we canned it for the last eighteen months. Then we decided that we needed to do something different for this tour so we put it back in. And we love playing it again. It was just great to play a song that you haven't played for a while again.

This'll probably change on a daily basis but I'm going to say that *End Over End* is the song that I'd give someone who was trying to get in to the Foos. Because it's long; you have to commit to listening to it and it touches on all the components that they cover as a band. You've got the solo intro and then it builds up in the middle and ends with a big, punchy outro. I'm trying to stay away from all the big hits and I think that I'm that B-Side guy that likes all the songs that nobody else likes! *These Days* will probably always be my favourite song. I don't know why it is but that song just grabbed me the first time I heard it and I've probably listened to it more times than any other song.

When it comes to being a fan at first my friends and family were like, "Well, he's in his late-teens so he's just going through a phase." But then I'm fortunate to have my Mum like the band and all my siblings kind of like them, too. My Dad like the band as well and I'm kind of blessed that it's not a weird band that they have some reason to detest. My friends all thought that it was a bit obsessive until we did what we did with the UK Foos. And then they all came flocking back and asking if I could put them on the guest list! I think they've got a filter these days and kind of block it out when I start talking about anything Foo related!

My band's recording soon once we've finished the songs that we're working on. I've had a couple of offers to join other bands but I'm just too busy at the moment! When the UK Foos finish and stop touring, then it'll be different. But right now my life is so consumed with rehearsing and touring. Hopefully the other band will take off at a convenient time because right now it's definitely not convenient! With the Foo, I'm hoping that, for their next album, they do what they do best; getting out an old tape machine and just jamming. *Wasting Light* was just the perfect album because they made it the way they wanted to make it despite the way the music industry was going and ended up coming out with these raw rock n' roll kind of sounds. I know that we got a couple of snippets of new songs at the Frome gig [February 2017] and it sounds like the Foo that we all want to hear.

I think that the band have got as long as they want; I don't think they're going to call it quits just yet. You look at similar bands; Black Sabbath were going for forty years, Rush were going for forty years, The Who were going for fifty years. Dave can keep writing the way he's writing. Taylor's forty six and he's still a phenomenal drummer. They can still do it. You look at all of Dave's mates; the Rolling Stone, KISS, and bands like that. They're all still going. So I think that Dave will take some kind of inspiration from his pals in KISS and think, "Well, if they can still do it then we can still do it.". Because they've got so many ideas and everyone's so fortunate that he's the front man because he's so creative and talented that he's always got material on the back burner. So, in my head, hopefully, they'll double what they've already done.

I don't have any Foos tattoos but I'm seriously considering getting Dave's *Sonic Highways*, "In the end we all come from what's come before" tattoo that he has on his forearm. I love that tattoo and as soon as he got it, I thought, "Oh my God, I want that!". If I was going to get one, I think that's what I'd get because it's indirectly Foo related because I'm basically ripping it off of Dave.

Hopefully music like that is still going to be around in fifty years time and if it's not thank God that they put the albums out when they did. I think that they're going to go down as one of the greats and it's kind of a blessing that Nirvana went the way that it did. Because maybe, if Kurt was still alive, the Foos wouldn't have happened. You never know, Dave Grohl may still be playing for Nirvana now. Everything seems to happen for some reason or another. Theirs is a pretty good legacy in that they've managed to keep going despite everything that's happened to them like Taylor nearly dying and members leaving and coming back. I think that even though they've gone through all of that and they're still making good albums and that they're still selling out shows all over the world means that they've staked their claim as a band that can be remembered for putting out good music.

# Kirri
## Newcastle, Australia

When I was little I bought a compilation album that comes out annually here in 'Straya for the Triple J Hottest 100 Countdown, and on that particular year, *This Is A Call* was on the list. So on tape 2, side 1, I got my first hit of Foo to the face.

Well, I think my conversion came in two stages - one was my first exposure via the tape as a kid, and the other was watching the video of their counter-protest against Westboro Baptist Church. I'd liked them for a long time but that was the thing that made me respect them a hell of a lot. I was totally sold on them from that day.

I'm going to stick with *This Is A Call* as the first song that I heard, but it's likely that I'd heard them on the radio in the background before that and just hadn't put two and two together. Let's say that was the one that had me sitting up with my ears pricked like a dog! *Wasting Light* was the first album that I went out and bought myself, but I could swear that I had a copy of *There Is Nothing Left to Lose* handed to me by a mate earlier than that (or stolen. That's likely, too.).

For me, they represent so many positive things that I search for in my experience of life beyond just enjoying a good tune. When I think of them, I think of joy, energy, creativity, humour, generosity, tenacity, friendship, and community. During some very dark times, their music has been a solace and a hand on the shoulder, like someone saying, "Come on, mate.". They've been a valuable example of shaping a world around your values and standing by them no matter what others might say or do. They remind me that there's no time or age limit on having fun and going for what you want.

I've joined in on the last two Aussie tours and seen them play in Sydney, Brisbane and Adelaide. I also made a last-minute trip up to the Gold Coast to see a Chevy Metal sunset gig on the beach, which was just a little bit special. Well, it's a harder slog between the US and Australia as opposed to Europe, so that's one of the reasons you guys in the UK see more of them! For us, the wait is a little longer between tours and appearances but we did get spoiled rotten on the *Wasting Light* release trail with the Goat Island show and the Manning Bar gig, plus we got a Chevy Metal show in between *Sonic Highways* dates teased right up to the last minute, so we've come to expect they've always got something up their sleeves. But the years between major tours can stretch pretty long, that's true. The internet and the whole discography keep the engine running, but the Aussie pocket of the Foo Family is a pretty close group of people. Many of us have bonded well beyond the band so we're constantly interacting in our daily lives. The music and the community keep me happy even when the band's in I-hate-us mode. Someone's got to keep the love going.

Getting to meet Taylor and Chris after that Chevy Metal show was the most brilliant end to my time following the tour from city to city. I was totally drilled by that point, caught a plane with less than 24 hours' notice, and got a B12 shot in the tush just to make it through. But being able to hug them and express my deepest appreciation for them made it all worth it. I also got to pitch in with a little bit of research for what turned out to be the first episode of *Sonic Highways*. Indirectly related to band stuff, being involved in the Foo community has led to friendships, overseas trips, and experiences that I'll hold in my heart forever.

My merch collection has become known as the "Fooseum" (okay, I started calling it that and it's grown from there)! I love collecting the rarities and oddities whenever I can manage it. The most obscure stuff I've found so far: A ticket from '98 signed by Franz and Taylor, one of the elusive *Sound City* cassettes (sent direct from the crew), an *In Your Honor* Post-It and pen promo set, a *24 Hours of Foo* talent pass, and a '97 UK tour itinerary. Someday, I'll have one of the original *Pocketwatch* tapes on the shelf. One sweet day when I'm cashed up.

It's actually about time to get a new display cabinet for the Fooseum because this one's getting a bit squishy! It started in a corner of my room and even as it grows it just feels natural to keep it in there. I live with two guys and the rest of my music collection's already dominating a lot of the space, plus this way it's protected from when house parties get sloppy.

I like finding the oddities and out-of-print stuff but there are a few things that are particularly special to me: Right up top is a *Sound City* mix tape that I got back in the the day that I've nicknamed 'Davesplosion', when the official Twitter account began following and interacting with people. I casually mentioned that I'd like to get my hands on one of those tapes and a DM popped up saying, "Nice t-shirt in your profile pic." (I was reppin' Taylor Hawkins and the Coattail riders). Shortly after, there it was in my mailbox. I also have a crew shirt from the Australia/NZ leg of the *In Your Honour* tour that I later found out through one of Taylor's long-time friends once belonged to him (neither of us have a clue how it wound up on eBay, but it's in the care of the Fooseum anyway). Then there's a special bundle I got on my last trip to the States, which was a pleasant surprise and one for which I'm utterly grateful, with a bunch of crew-only and promo swag (tour shirts, AAA passes, a glowing power block that was never put in the store and other goodies). All of this is pretty dope but it's also a testament to what quality people the band has working with them. Everyone onboard seems to be looked after, and in turn, they treat fans seriously well, too. Snaps for them.

I wish I could say I'm gifted to make my own merch, but the best I could come up with was painting custom text on t-shirts to wear to concerts. Even then, it looked like I'd done it while I was drunk. So I'd better leave it to someone who knows their shit.

The more I got involved with the band and the fans, the more I came to realise what I wanted to do with my time on this lil' blue planet. So I packed in my previous work and now I'm training up to become a counsellor. It came about because being a fan was making me aware of what existed beyond myself, and reminding me that human connection is what I value the most in this life. I think when a band can positively influence you beyond your relationship with music, that's when you know they're pretty special.

Writing for Foo Fighters Live is something I took up in late 2016 when Simon put out a call for interested writers to join the team. I was a freelance music writer for almost a decade so I was up for it, but what made me hurl myself at the opportunity was being able to pitch in with a site that's been such a wealth of knowledge for countless people. To this day, I still refer to it when I draw a blank on a date or recording detail. So in part, it was an obvious way I could show appreciation for all that hard work and pitch in however I could to keep the momentum going. The same could be said for how I approach contributing to the community as well – we're such a collaborative group. No one's particularly stingy with info or resources; no one actually cares whether you've been around for two months or two decades. When we see that you're enthusiastic about Foo Fighters, what's ours is yours.

As for other projects…I have an ongoing project, 'Things You Might Have Missed', appearing on my blog when time allows, which studies the details of Foo Fighters' music videos and discusses details and behind-the-scenes stories that elaborate on what we're seeing and add to the experience. As we speak, I'm about to rally the troops here in Australia in response to Chris teasing that he might be up for bringing a solo tour down to us if he sees that we're keen. I've had a couple of bigger ideas that are far more elaborate and would mean getting a lot of people behind them, but I'm letting them marinate for a bit longer!

I don't think it's a stretch to say that every fan with internet access can call themselves a beneficiary of Simon and co.'s tireless services. This would also be a great time to give a shout-out to Simon's book *7 Corners*, which documented Dave and Foo Fighters' entire known recording history up until its release in 2013. I'm still gobsmacked by the depth of details on every session. I definitely think it's important to have a comprehensive document because, besides being one of the biggest modern rock bands, they're also one of the hardest working bands who have become known for their ideology and technical approaches. It's a valuable thing to do as a fan to look at their methods and understanding the circumstances in which these recordings were made. With the listings for their live performances, it helps to paint a bigger picture of how they've evolved and, even just geographically, how far their music has reached. Once people get into that, I reckon it becomes evident that every bit of their success has been hard-earned. I'm not even being biased here. Maybe a little.

The band's legacy on my life? One word: Evolution. How would I describe them to someone? "You know that little skip your heart does when your plane's ready for take-off and the pilots crank that sucker up? That."

YOU DON'T KNOW WHAT YOU'RE ASKING WHEN YOU ASK ME TO PICK ONE SONG! Jeez, if I really had to pick just one song that represented a lot of what these guys can do, I guess I'd have to say *The Pretender* because it showcases the best of everything.

My closest friends don't share the same level of enthusiasm as I do, but we've all got different tastes that sometimes overlap so it's no biggy. They love and accept me as I am. I grew up in a musical household (my dad's a musician himself) so it hasn't taken much to get them onboard. Plus they learned a long time ago that when it comes to music, don't even question it, just let it happen. (Dad's a big fan of *Wheels*. So that's one other person outside Germany who's feeling it.)

Most of the time, the second I announce myself as a Foo fan, one of two things happen: Either the person I'm talking to will pick up what I'm putting down, or someone else within earshot will jump in and want to start talking about them! I've found that even if someone doesn't call Foo Fighters their favourite band, there's still a level of appreciation and respect for what they've contributed to rock history. I did go to a birthday dinner with a guy who hates Foo Fighters with a burning passion. We took it outside. Kidding. Maybe.

I used to be in a drumming troupe and I'll bash one out if it's feeling good (cough), but I haven't played seriously for a few years. Nowadays I tend to just watch Dave and Taylor drum, mouth wide in awe, eyes narrowed with envy.

I've had a Foo related tattoo in the works for a while but haven't gotten around to getting the actual ink done yet. A good friend and I will share the same design (she got the jump on me) - an altered version of the bomb/wings design from the *Echoes, Silence, Patience, and Grace* era, with the words 'Destroy/Rebuild'. I think those words sum up what it's been like to kick it with this band and how things have changed as a result of that. Along those lines, I've also thought about getting the words "as long as I can fight, I'll survive".

I think they'll be remembered for being one of the bands that really went the distance and brought the rock when people were writing rock off. They'll be the example that future generations refer to when they speak of how music has evolved in present day, and yet there have been a handful of acts who have been unwilling to compromise or be phased out. Many of their songs will become timeless classics - it's already happening, with tracks recorded twenty years ago finding new audiences because the music still speaks to so many. I like to think they'll be celebrated as being one of the last champions of the human element. (Is there any way to say "human element" without snickering? If there is, teach me.)

Just to say that I don't think I've laughed as much with, or felt as close to, a group of fans as much as I have with the Foo community. The way that people from all walks of life look out for one another is something seriously special. You're all top-shelf. High fives all around.

# Nik
## Windsor, UK

I'm probably not the oldest Foo Fighters fan. I'm 33 and, while I'm younger than the band, I'm probably a lot older than some of the new fans. I really got into the Foo Fighters because I fell in love with Nirvana first. Obviously, after Kurt passed, I got in to the Foo Fighters. They're a band where Dave Grohl is a massive focal point and it's built around him. He openly admitted to me that if it hadn't been for Nirvana there would have been no Foo Fighters. I've always had a lot of respect for him how, after Nirvana ended, to have the balls to start the Foo Fighters. It's not the same band [as Nirvana]. But there's definitely a similarity in terms of genre, vibe, and how to approach writing and crafting a song. So I think that the Foo Fighters, and Dave in particular, are not only a big inspiration but that I also appreciate what they do and how they do it. They're always a band that wants to give back and a lot of what I've learned about recording a live band is from watching what they've done. That's one of the things I most enjoy about them. They want to share and they want to inspire other people. One thing I definitely picked up from meeting them is that they're very encouraging of people writing music and creating songs and being in bands and keeping live music alive. Because of that,

I've always been a fan.

I first saw the Foos when my Dad took me to see them. They played the Shepard's Bush Empire on *The Colour and the Shape* tour. It was their second album, right after Taylor Hawkins joined the band. We got tickets at the door and I was very young, maybe 13 or 14. Then it became a life ambition to meet Dave Grohl and have a chat. I just wanted to meet him and show my appreciation for what he's done and why he did it. I'm a part time musician myself and I've always played in original bands. I've just been in the studio working on an album and I always think that it's good to pay tribute to the artists that inspired you.

I'm a bit of a strange, quirky guy and what I ended up doing, a long time ago, was I'd saved up some money and I decided to build a guitar. Kurt commissioned Fender to him a custom guitar that was a hybrid between a Mustang and a Fender Jaguar. They called it a "Jagstang" but he never actually played it because he died before the guitar was finished. So what I did was, by putting different parts together, I built my own Fender Jagstang guitar. But I had it painted in Dave Grohl's Gibson Pelham Blue colours. It was the guitar that I always played with. I gigged with it in my Nirvana tribute band and I even used it in a Foo Fighters tribute band. Life just carried on and I did my thing. The Foo Fighters were about to release *Sonic Highways* and in London they were doing a show for Prince Harry [The Invictus Games]. I got tickets to that show but I heard that, on September 11th [2014] under the name The Holy Shits, they were doing a secret show in a small skate club in London. It was open to only industry people and only two hundred fan tickets were sent out. On the day I heard about it I said, "Fuck it. I'm going to go down without a ticket and without an invite. I'll put the [Jagstang] guitar in my car.". When I built it I always had the intention that, if I ever met Dave, I'd give it to him as a gift.

I got to the venue and, obviously, they told me that I wasn't invited and nor was I on the guest list. So I said to them, "Is it okay to hang back until after the show?". And they were fine with that. So what I did, because it was in an underpass in London, was I just chilled out. I pulled out the guitar and started jamming *The Pretender*. One of the bouncers called me over and said, "Actually, you can come in.".

I went in and I watched the show and it was really good. Obviously, they didn't play anything off *Sonic Highways* but right at the end of the show they finished with the opening to *Something From Nothing*. After the show finished, everyone's clearing out and I'm heading for the front. I spoke to a bouncer and asked if it would be possible to meet Dave. He sent me to talk to another guy who told me to talk to another guy. So I go and talk to this bouncer. Seriously, he was like seven foot tall. I told him, "I'm here to meet Dave Grohl. I've got a guitar with me to give to him as a gift.". And he told me, "Well, you want to talk to that guy over there. That's Dave's manager.". So I walked over to this gentleman and I said, "Hi. You must be John Silva.". He turned round to me and said, "How the hell do you know that? No one knows who I am.". And I told him, "That guy I'd just spoken to had said that you're Dave Grohl's manager, which must make you John Silva 'cause you managed Nirvana and I know that you manage the Foo Fighters.". He laughed his head off and said that it had happened to him a week before when Prince Harry had come up to him and said, "You must be John Silva." and I was only the second person, after Prince Harry, to say the same thing! So I spoke to him about the show and told him who I am and why I'm there. I said that I had a guitar for Dave and he [John] was a really, really nice gentleman. He told me to hang back with him and that, after everyone had cleared out, he'd take me backstage to meet Dave. It was quite inspiring that I went out on the cuff and ended up meeting the band. It was quite amazing because it was always a life ambition to meet Dave and the band.

It was quite an enlightening experience in a way. I walked in to the room, and walked straight past Dave because he was surrounded by people and I just hung back and chilled out. Taylor Hawkins was stood right in front of me. He was a really nice guy. I told him a bit about who I am and why I'm there and he was said, "Oh, you didn't make me a drum set?! You made Dave a guitar but didn't make me a drum set?". We had a bit of a joke. He's one of the best drummers who's ever played and the only reason I had a photo of him was 'cause he's a dude from California and I'm a refugee from Yugoslavia and sooner or later we ran out of things to talk about. So I said, "How about we take a picture?" and he asked a photographer to take a photo of us on my phone. Then John came back and told me that Dave was going to come over and talk to me.

He came over and we spoke for about ten or fifteen minutes. I told him what I'd made and he was was really thankful and really excited. He even took it out of the bag. At that point Pat Smear, who's a really cool guy, walked over and said, "Oh, wow. That's Kurt's Jagstang.".

We spoke about music. They asked what I did and I told them that I played in a Foo Fighters tribute band and a Nirvana tribute band. I showed Dave my Foo Fighters tattoo. I have a lyric from *Best of You* tattooed on to my hand and he showed me his latest one, which is lyrics from *Something From Nothing*. He's a very humble man who I felt is someone who's not afraid to be himself or to be real. I think when you see him in interviews and on stage, he's definitely an amazing performer and larger than life character. But when you meet him on a one to one level, he's very humble, very sincere, and very honest.

We even started discussing the set list for the Invictus Games. I remember saying to him, "As long as you open with *All My Life*, you'll be fine.". Funnily, when I saw the show, they opened with *All My Life*. They would probably have opened with it anyway, but it was really amazing to think that maybe I'd influenced that decision a little.

At the time, I was mixing that first album that I made. I'd finished mixing two songs that I put in the guitar case for him to listen to. What was funny was that he said that, years ago, he took apart a guitar and he's never been able to put it back together. He made a joke to Pat that maybe he should send me the guitar. I said that I'd definitely put it back together for him. Unfortunately, I'm still waiting for this guitar! I live my life thinking that, any day now, I'm going to get Dave Grohl's guitar through the post!

I definitely got on with Dave the best out of all of the band. We had a really interesting conversation about song writing and music. The whole experience meant a lot to me and, as I left the club, the bouncer that initially let me in asked me where my guitar was. I told him that I gave it to Dave Grohl and thanked him for letting me in.

In one night I fulfilled a life ambition. For me, being a lifelong fan, the reception I got from their manager, from Taylor, Pat, and Dave, was amazing. Some people say that you shouldn't meet your heroes. I definitely felt like it was a good thing for me to meet them. Although it was short lived, in those ten to fifteen minutes, I made a friend. From the way he writes the songs, from the way he delivers his lyrics, and the emotion he puts in it, I always felt that we would connect on that very human level. So it was a very moving evening. Not just the concert, although it was always a dream of mine to see the Foo Fighters in a very small club. And the time they gave me afterwards truly was memorable and special. Obviously, I told Dave that I made the guitar as a thank you for carrying on what Nirvana started and keeping the genre alive, all be it with a new band.

They're very supportive of carrying on writing your own music and not just being a musician who plays in cover bands. It feels like there's something left unsaid or unfinished in one way 'cause he was quite keen for me to hang out and chat more about music. But sadly that never happened. It doesn't leave me feeling a sense of regret 'cause I definitely felt like I got what I came for. I wanted to go and say thank you and they gave me the time for that so I couldn't really ask for any more.

The second album, that I've just finished recording, is much better than the first album that I was creating at that time. We've just finished recording it, myself and my drummer, and we've just sent it off to the producer to be mixed, mastered, and have additional instrumentation added. It's a massive step up and I definitely think this album has partly been written

61

because of the meeting and the inspiration they gave me.

My band, From Day One, started from my Nirvana tribute band. I decided that I'd form my own Nirvana tribute band and the first step was to find a drummer who could play as well as Dave Grohl. Eventually I put out an advert looking for a drummer and I said that I'd be interested in doing some original music as well as covers and someone responded. We jammed a couple of Nirvana songs and it clicked [between us] so we started playing and writing together. The first album was made, on a very low budget, while the Nirvana tribute was doing its thing. We wanted to record some songs and I did it myself. Out of that, we found someone to manage it and put it out there. It was with the arrangement that we'd make a better [second] record, which was in the pipeline at the time. However, I'd been trying to make it in bands for a long, long time so I don't really do it with dreams of it being a massive success. It's more to get stuff out there, and to have something to say. When you have the ability to write and create music it's like any art form in that you have a way to express yourself and to leave something behind. I think that's what the best music and the best art does; to allow an artist to say what they want, the way they want to say it, and inspire people to challenge others in the way they think or the way want to create something.

The world has changed massively since the dawn

of the internet. The music industry has changed completely because of it. I'm quite indifferent to the music business. I think it's definitely harder for musicians to make money and to get themselves out there. But it's not something that really bothers me. I think that if, these days, you're making music to make money then you've got a few wires crossed and that you need to rethink why you're making music. People who make music these days usually make it because they want to create. And maybe that's a good thing in a way 'cause it really should give birth to better art coming out. There's always going to be a need for good music, good bands, and good artists to exist. It's important that people keep creating.

It's pretty much the same thing that Taylor Hawkins said to me. The Foo Fighters have pretty much the same ethos and it is important because whenever you're creating a new song, you're challenging things.

I did guitar lessons at school from between the ages of about nine and thirteen. When I went to high school, I used to go to an after school youth club where they did a rock school. There was a guy who used to write for *Guitarist* magazine who would get us together every Tuesday night for two or three hours. Loads of young kids would come with guitars, basses, and drum kits and he would pick a song and then make a band out of it. Although he wasn't a classically trained musician he really taught me a lot about how you construct bands and how you make arrangements. From a very young age I started playing and jamming in original bands, trying to get somewhere. Subsequently, I've gone on to do other things and I wouldn't say that music is how I make my money but it's always something that's part of me. Although it's not something that's allowed me to make a living, it's been something that has given me a route to express myself.

I play a Gretsch guitar that came out this year [2016]. It's the first Gretsch semi-hollow body, very similar to the ES335, and it comes with a stock bridge. I bought the guitar with a hard case for £300. The Gretsch Streamliner is what it's called and it's a great sounding guitar. I play that through a Fender Twin, which is what I've always used, and it's my favourite guitar amp. Other than that, for a back up guitar I have a Fender Jaguar, but I don't really play anything else. I also recently bought a ukulele to learn to play it. I took it in to the studio and added some ukulele overdubs to this album. The studio guys loved it so we kept them!

What's the Foos song that I'd recommend to people so that they could get in to the band? I think the tattoo that I have on my arm, *Were you born to resist or be abused. I swear I'll never give in. I refuse. Best of You*, is their best song. I said that to Dave. I remember when I showed him my tattoo. He turned to me and said, "It's a shame that I don't have so many lyrics that are worth a tattoo.". And I was like, "I think you're wrong, mate. I think you've written a lot better stuff than you realise.".

How would I describe the band to someone who'd never heard them before? I think "epic" would be a good way to put it. They genuinely have a lot of epic songs. I think the sound is full of raw energy and sound and the lyrics can almost be haunting at times, really challenging you to question and think. They have such a wide variety of songs that they've written and I definitely wouldn't put them in the box of a genre. You could say that they're a hard rock band but then they did the acoustic show [*Skin and Bones*]. They're one of the biggest bands in the world and one of the reasons that they are is because they've produced at such a high quality for so long. They're a band that started and built its way up. Definitely Nirvana gave it [Foo Fighters] a stepping stone but it still had to build up, the numbers [of fans] still had to grow, and the venues that they played still had to get larger and larger. And that's something that you only achieve over time.

The coolest thing of theirs that I own is a beach bag. It doesn't even say the Foo Fighters; it says The Holy Shits. It was the poster from that secret show I went to and they were handing them out at the show. That's got to be the most unusual piece of merchandise that I own.

I think that their legacy will depend on a lot and it

will be a positive one. That much I can say. Obviously a lot of it will be down to Dave. He's the front man of the band, he's the chief songwriter and it all comes through him. I think anyone who comes in to contact with Dave and the band always comes away feeling positive about it. I think their legacy will be them being remembered for creating a lot of positivity and joy, as well as for creating really powerful music that delivered a lot of passion and bought out the best in us.

# Toni
Kentucky, USA

I really don't remember how I discovered the band. I do remember enjoying them when they first came out on the radio. When David Letterman had his heart surgery, I was working nights and I believe I remember them being on the first show after Letterman had his surgery. I remember him making a comment about the name of the band, 'Foo Fighters, they fight foo' or whatever, and making a crack about it. The main memory that stands out is I remember hearing *Learn to Fly* on the radio and thinking, "I really like that song.". I was shopping with some friends of mine and we were in a store and that song came on and I just stopped in the middle of the store, thinking "I love this song!".

The first albums I owned were copies that a friend in Texas made for me in October 2010. I got *One By One*, *There's Nothing Left to Lose*, the first self-titled album, and I think, *The Color and the Shape*. I bought *Echoes, Silence, Patience, and Grace* second-hand while in Texas. When *Wasting Light* came out I couldn't afford very much of anything and so a friend in Canada felt bad for me and sent it to me. She kind of became a fan through me and she was like, "Oh, their new album's out.". And I said, "Yeah, I know, I want it so bad but I can't afford to buy the extra stuff.". So she bought it and sent it to me.

The band mean a lot to me. I love their music. I've always loved music and I'm one of those people who can remember all the words to *American Pie* but I can't remember to pay my electric bill on time. Some people are movie fans, which I can take or leave. Music really affects me on so many levels. I love that the guys don't take themselves too seriously. We have Hawkins Hair on Twitter, which is hilarious. I love that they don't seem to let success go to their heads. They just look at themselves as goofy nerds who got lucky and making a lot of money for doing what they love. They seem to remember what it's like to be a fan and still act like fans. Like, they have Brian May's underwear hanging in their studio. There's footage of Dave dancing at the music awards with his red Solo cup. They obviously work their assess off for their fans. A good example of that is when Dave broke his leg. They could have very easily have said, "Okay, we're cancelling the whole tour.". But I'm sure that their thinking was more like, "Well, we've got all these fans that we don't want to disappoint." and they figured out a way to make the tour work with Dave's broken leg. So there's like a mutual love and respect between the band and the fans. Their performances reflect how much they love doing what they do. One of the things I absolutely love is watching Pat. He stands there with this big smile on his face and my goal in life is to love my life, and my job, as much as Pat obviously loves his.

I've come close to seeing the Foos live twice. The first time was when I got screwed over by getting a fake ticket to the Ryman [31$^{st}$ October 2014]. The second time was when I was going to see them in Nashville for the stadium show but I got sick and had to cancel. I did get to California to see Chevy Metal play at Conejo Valley Days and I really loved it. It was heaven on Earth! Conejo Valley Days is really low key, basically like a county fair. The whole experience of seeing Chevy Metal was awesome. The band brought up people that they had met before and had them play. They had that one little ten year old boy playing the drums and you could see Taylor standing in front, cheering him on.

I've made some great friends through fan sites. I look at the Foo Family site once in a while. My friends run Taylor Hawkins Shorts and I'm also a member of The Birds of Satan fan page. I have fifteen Foos shirts. I have one special shirt that I helped to design which says "Popping My Foo Fighters Cherry". I was going to wear it to go and see my first concert but that fell through. I have three Chevy Metal shirts, three Birds of Satan shirts, and a Taylor Hawkins and the Coattail Riders shirt. I have nine of their DVDs and three Foo related bumper stickers on my car. Someone got the

Nashville poster for me. Through one fan site I got some pictures of the guys. Someone took photos and printed them and I framed those. My most favourite thing is a picture of Taylor that a friend of mine took at Love Ride 2015. She printed it and somebody had Taylor sign it and I got it for Christmas. I do have a silver infinity symbol ring that I bought when *Sonic Highways* came out and I wear it every day.

Music has always been really influential to me and has a special place in my heart. The Foos music has really touched me. There's some of their songs that really speak to me and the Foos haven't been any exception to that. I feel like I will always be a fan and will always look forward to whatever they do in the future.

Basically, the Foos are rock n' roll. They're definitely not cookie cutter music and they have a little something for everybody. They're like a musical buffet. One day I was playing *White Limo* at work and one of my co-workers walked by my desk. I had the speakers on but I didn't have it turned up real loud and she asked, "What the Hell are you listening to?". And I said, "This is actually Foo Fighters, too.".

It depends on what kind of music someone likes in general. If they like the heavier stuff, *White Limo* or *The Pretender*. Otherwise, I'd have them listen to *Learn to Fly* or *Times Like These* which are two of my personal favourites.

I think my friends and family are used to me being

a little crazy and over enthusiastic about music. One co-worker made the comment that I'm like a teenager again because I'm always talking about the music and the band. I rotate photos of Foo Fighters and/or Taylor as my computer wallpaper. I talk about the band *a lot*. My friends respect that I have a lot of enthusiasm and put up with the fact that when they get in my car there's probably going to be a Foo Fighters song playing on the CD player.

I think that their music will always be listened to. I think it'll last because they're not your run of the mill band and they've lasted over twenty years so far. I hope that they'll be studied as the group that grew. Kind of like Madonna. She grew and evolved. I'm hoping that fifty years from now people are taking a music class and are learning that if you want to last then you have to change with the times. That's what the Foos have done.

# Stefano
## Rome, Italy
(Documentary Film-maker – Dreaming of Foo Fighters)

There were many things that happened. First of all, in 2011 there was the *Wasting Light* tour and I had tickets for the concert here in Italy. And the day of the concert, my daughter was born and I have a beautiful photograph [with her] where I have that Foo Fighters t-shirt with *In Your Honor* on it. Because of her birth, I did not attend the concert. In that period, I worked with some guys for a musical project and I discovered that one of them had a Foo Fighters tribute band. So I listened to his music because he recorded a demo of three songs in his studio.

There is also the question of passion. Passion, for me, is a good value in a group or person. In my professional work I sometimes make changes to my life because I was an architect, and after that an art director before becoming a photographer. All the things that I did, I did only because I was following my passion. With the Foo Fighters, when you see them doing the Garage Tour you know that they weren't doing it for the money but for the feeling of playing with a few people instead of somewhere like Wembley. I decided to make this trip through the fans because getting in touch with the Foo Fighters is impossible. I discovered a lot of fans, a lot of tribute bands, and I decided to make this movie. This is my first movie and I had no money, I had no experience, and I decided to make it all by myself because if I had people that helped me then this project may never be finished. I didn't know if I'd ever be able to make a movie as it's a big project with an hour long narrative structure. You have to write and direct something. It's huge. But you do it step by step.

Making the movie was very tough and there were many times when I wanted to quit because it was too much for one person with no experience. I really didn't know how to get it made. There was another little problem, or question, for me because of the value of passion. I have a five year old daughter and the big question for me was what I want for her when she's older. Hopefully she will follow her passion. That was the turning point of that movie because I have to face myself. Because my project was to describe a situation that I see and I decided to put myself in it. My choice originally wasn't to be in it but I needed to be to tell the story as I saw it.

I don't know if the documentary will ever get a release date. If you make the movie you may end up with nothing because you have huge hurdles to overcome along the way. I knew that when I started the movie. I said to myself, "If I have to fix the copyright problem before I make the movie, I will never make it because I'm not a legal person and I'm not a producer. There are a lot of problems with contacting people to get the right permissions. I'm not a big production company. I'm just Stefano!". When you call Sony, no one will reply.

For that reason, I decided that I would make this movie alone. Even if it never gets released, it's okay because my dream is to make the movie. It's the first step. I had a little contact with the management because I tried to contact them in a lot of ways; email, phone calls, gifts. In November [2015], the Foo Fighters were in Italy and I saw them in Bologna. A friend of mine that lives in Bologna told me to get my phone because he was walking through the city and, if he met Dave Grohl, he'd call me. And it happened! I spoke with him and he didn't know anything about the movie because the news never got to him. I asked him, "How do I get my movie to you?". His answer was perfect. He said, "I don't know. Maybe some day you'll find out.".

After that phone call, I sent an email to the management. The point behind the email was that I'd just spoken with Dave Grohl about getting the movie to him. After this email, Michael, a very good person, replied to me. They all knew about a guy in Italy that had made this movie. He wrote to me and told me that there was a problem with the legal side but nothing came from it. Last month [June 2016], I sent him another email with the finished movie and he watched the preview of it. In August [2016], I will be in Los Angeles and I told him that the preview he saw was the final movie and that I would be in Los Angeles if he wanted to speak about the copyright. I have to face these problems as the international copyright is too much for me to deal with on my own.

Making the movie was a good experience for me. I've never been to cinema school so I've never learned the art of making movies. But, at the moment, I can't put the movie on the internet for everyone to see because of the music. The songs aren't original songs but it is the Foos music as played by tribute bands. And some of the fans spoke about Wembley so I put in some of the footage of the Foo Fighters playing Wembley. Of course, there is a huge world of legal issues that go with it!

I've always loved the band but the turning point was *Wasting Light*. The album is awesome. His documentary about the making of *Wasting Light* [*Back and Forth*] because there was the idea about making the album in Dave's garage and then doing the Garage Tour is so perfect. It was the vision of doing something different and then working on that idea in the best way possible. They have wonderful songs but, for me, there is this part about passion. It's the attitude with how they go about making their albums and, for me, it's really important. All of them came from the punk community and, when you come from that, you play on a little stage for just the people in the club. For me, that's the same spirit that they still have.

The Foo Fighters concert last year [2015] was like a

huge party! It was a lot of fun because it felt more like a party than a concert. I also saw them in Washington DC because I won a ticket for the second date of the *Sonic Highways* surprise shows [October 24th 2014]. It was the first thing that I've ever won in my life! I saw them in a small club [the Black Cat] with 350 people, and the band played for three hours. It was great because, before the concert, we watched the Washington DC episode of *Sonic Highways*. It was very different because I've seen the Foo Fighters at a big venue in Italy and a very small club in Washington DC. They were both very good but in Washington DC it felt like going to see a friend's band play. They're a fun band.

When I was working on that movie, I didn't know that the *Sonic Highways* album had been made along with the eight documentaries! I hope that Foo Fighters will be remembered for their great music as well as for the many ideas that they have and the way that they produce them. This will stay with people because *Sonic Highways*, where they recorded a song in eight different cities, is not a mainstream concept. I think that's the part about them that's very genuine.

# Nikki
## Liverpool, UK

I was always aware of Dave Grohl because my partner, Chris, who I've been with since I was fifteen, absolutely loves Nirvana. Because of him, I knew of the Foo Fighters and Chris played me some of their stuff. I remember saying to him [Chris], at the time, "All he does is scream. I don't understand what the fascination with him is."! I think, at the time, I was in to a lot of pop music. It was around 2008 when I changed jobs and was able to listen to the radio. I was listening to Chris Moyles's show and Dave Grohl was on as a guest. They were playing bits of songs and I was thinking, "I know that song. I know that song.". And he [Dave] seemed like a really nice guy and came across really well. It was basically from listening to that radio show that I listened to some of their [Foo Fighters] albums and watched some interviews and thought, "Yeah, I really like these guys". It was from then that I really got in to them.

The first album I bought was *One By One* and the first song that I remember hearing was *Times Like These*. It's my favourite song of all time!

Personally, without wanting to sound cliché and with what I've been through with my health, it's not just a band to me any more. They've become a lot more personal than that and their music helped me through a lot of really, really bad times, a lot of treatments, and a lot of physio. That was my goal. I was in a wheelchair for ten months and, through listening to them, that was my aim; I had to get better because I was going to go and see them. So it was certain songs that really resonated and struck a chord with me. I like a lot of bands and went to a lot of festivals before I got ill but I don't think I've ever connected with a band quite like I have with the Foo Fighters. The songs that meant the most were *Times Like These*, *No Way Back*, *Best of You*, and *Walk*, obviously. It was those songs that helped me through my illness.

I saw them for the first time in 2015 at Milton Keynes Bowl. We were supposed to see them at Wembley but then it all went tits up when Dave broke his leg. That was sort of the irony that I got out of it all! I'd gotten out of a wheelchair to go and see them and then he broke his leg! I was like, "For the love of God, I will get to see this band at some point!". I was ill for quite a few years and then circumstances before that, time off work and things like that, we couldn't get it together to go and see them. I was thinking, "I'm finally getting to see them! ...oh no... No, I'm not.". We still ended up travelling to London because we were going to lose the money [on hotels booked for Wembley] and we ended up going and seeing the UK Foo Fighters that put on that little gig next to Wembley Stadium. And the amount of people that I saw on crutches and with their legs in plaster at that gig was funny. At the time, I was on my sticks and we were all asking each other what we'd done to end up on crutches! I've never known so many people with their legs in casts!

I've made lots of friends over Twitter because of the band. You know, people you message and chat to about day to day things. There's a lady on Twitter called Debbie who I've really connected with. Her Mum's family are from Liverpool and it's the little things like that that really mean something. So it's been over Twitter and social media that I've met people and they all seem to have a story to tell of how they got in to the band. Foo Fighters fans are so lovely. I can't tell you how many gigs and festivals I've been to over the years and you get some really, really nasty fans. They say they're fans but they're just out to get pissed and cause trouble. But there's this atmosphere [with Foo Fighters fans] that everyone's just out to have a good time. Everyone's happy to help and they want to know why you're there, where you come from, and who you're with. It's just a lovely atmosphere.

I've got a handmade, wooden plaque with some of the words from *Everlong* on. It's up in the kitchen. I got a couple of bits from someone in Virginia who was making custom Break A Leg tour wristbands. As for official merchandise, I've got the usual stuff. T-shirts, wristbands, badges, a couple of setlists that I've had mounted. Just the general bits and bobs. There's the stuff that family have given me; there's a phone case and an iPad case. I can't really go too mad because we've only got a small house and I don't really want Chris getting jealous with Dave Grohl's face everywhere! I'm waiting for the tea towels to come back in stock. They're bright orange with a silhouette print of Dave's face on them. Not to use, obviously, because I'm not going to dry my dirty dishes on Dave Grohl's face!

The band's lasting legacy for me is that they've helped me through tough times and got me through the other side. That sounds really cringe worthy doesn't it?! But you know when you hear some people talk about bands and you think, "Get over yourself. It's just a band."? I can understand it now because I've been through it myself.

I literally beat up my partner about going to see the Foos. We'd been to Milton Keynes Bowl to see The Prodigy a few years back. When the Foos announced the dates, he said, "You're not going to be able to manage that on your sticks.". I told him that I didn't care what they had to do to get me there, I am going! This is what I'd worked through all my treatments and physio for and I was getting there. And I did it! I hounded him the night before by telling him that we were going in the pit. He told me that I couldn't and I said, "Watch me!". I'd told him that the aim was to get back in the pit. I did it and it was just unreal. I lost one of my crutches but it was worth it! We didn't make it to the rail but we were about three rows back from the end of the runway.

I'd say that the Foo Fighters are the best band in the world. People don't get an option with me; they know about the band whether they want to or not! If I was trying to get someone interested in the band, the one song I'd give them would be *Times Like These*.

I think my friends and family think I'm a little bit strange for being a fan of the band! Only because when I was younger, I was so much in to boy bands. My younger brother took me to see Muse and that was the start of my love affair with rock music. Everyone basically thinks I'm nuts! My family know how much I love the band and they just laugh. Other friends are quite shocked because I'm a very private person and they'd never expect me to be into that type of music. There were a few videos that surfaced on my partner's phone of me in the pit. People were saying, "In the name of God, you were using those sticks like pogo sticks!". I was screaming, and shouting, and wolf whistling. My brother in law actually said, "Jesus Christ, it's like watching a twelve year old at a One Direction concert."! I did make a bit of a show of myself. But it took a lot for me to get there! I was going to enjoy it!

But it was a lot more than going to see a band. It was a lot more than going to see a concert. We never ever thought I'd walk again. Not only had I got out of a wheelchair and out of a zimmer frame but I lost my speech as well so I had to go through intensive speech therapy as well. I lost vision in my left eye. It was a lot more than just being in a wheelchair. Like I said, it was a lot more than going to a concert; it was two and a half years of sheer hell, physio, and treatments to get there. So it was a big, big deal.

I don't have a Foo Fighters tattoo yet but I am planning on having one. I'm thinking of having of having the double F – the Foo Fighters logo – on the back of my neck.

What will the Foos legacy be in fifty years time? The greatest rock band in the world.

# Simon
England
(Admin for **Foo Fighters Live**)

As far as I recall I first heard the band on the radio, as you did in the pre-internet days for any artist, I guess. They got played on the 'regular' shows during the day but there was also a special 'Rock Show' that I used to listen to each week on Radio 1. For the most part they played heavier artists but they did throw in the odd Foo track. I still have cassettes with recordings I made of the show!

I've been a fan, I guess, since around 1999 when I first heard them, when I would have been 12 years old. I was a full-on fan within a year or two. I don't know what the actual first song I heard was but the first I remember was *Monkey Wrench*. I just loved the tempo, the screaming bit, it was nothing like the pop/chart songs that you usually heard. *Hey, Johnny Park!* was also an early favourite, although I labelled it on one of my tapes as *Every Blue* (I misheard the lyric 'Your every mood').

If I remember correctly, I got the first three albums all at the same time, around 2000/2001, as a gift. It was quite the treat, to finally just hear all this music, having only heard the singles that aired on the radio to that point. After that I received, or bought, each album at release. It's been such a long time I don't really know which of the three I liked most to begin

83

with but I'd guess *The Color And The Shape* because I liked the loud, 'screamy' songs.

Music in general is a huge part of my life and Foo Fighters are a key part of that as one of my favourite artists. Listening to their music can positively affect you in so many ways, making you happy, cheering you up or just making you want to head bang and rock the air guitar (or drums, as I usually prefer!). It's obviously not just the music though. The guys are all so likeable, down to earth characters that make loving the band so much easier. They're always so good to their fans with what they offer and have fun teasing us in various ways with cryptic websites or even mysterious invitations in the post.

I've seen them live nine times since 2006. I had hoped, and wanted, to see them on their 2002 and 2005 UK tours but circumstances meant it didn't work out with not being old enough to go on my own at the time. Once I finally could go on my own it was certainly worth the wait! Venues have varied from Wembley Stadium with 85,000 other fans to the House Of Vans, an 850 capacity venue under the famous Waterloo station in London. Each venue and concert has its own memories for different reasons, but any live show is a great experience. The atmosphere, the energy, the human element of a live performance and, of course, being there in great company. Whether singing along and jumping up and down with 85,000 people or 850, you can't beat it.

I've not really got any special stories relating to them but I have met a lot of good friends because of the band. A large part of that is thanks to their online message board, a place for fans to discuss anything and everything about the band. I'm a very shy person generally and so the idea of meeting strangers from the internet will always be daunting to me, so much so that the first time I went to a Foo Fighters show I was a few feet behind a group of people I knew were from the Postboard but I was too scared to go up and say hello!

I eventually did get up the courage to meet up with a group of Postboard fans a little later and it couldn't have gone any better. There are people from all over the United Kingdom (and in fact other countries) that I can now consider my friends solely thanks to Foo Fighters. We all of course share a passion for the band and it makes going to a show all the more fun.

I guess you could say I have a fairly large collection of Foo Fighters merchandise that consists of several hundred CDs, vinyl records, photos, and more. Some of my most treasured items include a drumstick used by Dave Grohl at a Them Crooked Vultures concert and a limited edition lithograph of the *Wasting Light* album cover that was hand signed by all five members of the band as of 2011 and sold as part of a special edition of the album.

Shortly before getting into Foo Fighters I got into Nirvana through friends at school. One of them had their live album, *From The Muddy Banks Of The Wishkah,* which I really enjoyed. Something about the raw sound of a live performance just appealed to me. This continued with Foo Fighters and, going back to recording from the radio, I have a rather worn out tape of one of their live shows broadcast on Radio 1 in 1999.

At some point, whilst looking for Nirvana related websites, I stumbled upon the website LiveNirvana.com. The site documented the live performance history of the band and recordings of those shows could be acquired via the forums. As mentioned above live recordings of any band just appealed to me more than studio albums and so this was quite the treasure trove, discovering the live history of a band that I was unfortunately a little too young to have known first hand.

It would therefore come as no surprise that a group of us decided we wanted to do the same for Foo Fighters. Websites already existed that documented their live tour history and we took on the mantle, ensuring the data was updated and added to. A couple of years into its existence I took sole ownership of the site and with my other passion, web development and design, the website basically became a hobby combining two of my interests. The primary reason for the site to exist is for other fans, hence the slogan we coined of "For the fans, by the fans". I continue to add new sections, new features, and ensure the information is freely available for as long as possible, for other fans to enjoy, including future generations.

I don't know if the band are aware of the site or what they think of it if they do, but I would hope they appreciate the dedication and passion I (and other contributors) have for them. This is also essentially what inspires me to keep it going; the passion I have for the band and keeping this 'service' available for all other fans of the band with a similar passion.

The band will probably always be part of my life even if, for any reason, my interest in them wanes in the future. They will always be a band that I have a passion for, a band that has given me so many memories over the years. As I said in a previous answer, music in general is a huge part of my life and I'm sure that will always be the case, and Foo Fighters, as a huge part of that, will always be there.

I guess I would describe them as a rock band with a little something for everyone. My mum, in her 50's, likes songs like *Skin And Bones* and *Wheels,* my sister, who usually likes pop/boy band types,  likes *Learn To Fly* and *My Hero* whilst I really love songs like *Wattershed* and *White Limo* which would leave them sticking fingers in their ears or in my mum's case, asking "What's this racket?!"

Their overall sound hasn't really changed that much over their 20+ year career but as I say, throughout their catalogue they really offer something for everyone. You could give anyone an album to start with depending on their preferences and there is a good chance they'd at least like some of what they hear.

You can't really go wrong with any of the big hits but as per my previous answer, what song you give them would really depend on what they like. If they like heavy stuff and come from the Nirvana fan groups, then I'd give them something from the first two records, maybe *Wattershed* or *My Poor Brain*. If they were into poppier stuff, maybe *Learn To Fly* or *Rope*. If I had to decide on one song that was quintessential Foo Fighters, I'd have to give the cliché answer of *Everlong*.

My friends and family obviously know I'm a bit of a nut about Foo Fighters. A lot of them like the band as well, or are huge fans of other artists, so I think they get it even if they can't understand why I'd want eight different copies of the same album!

I try not to talk about the band too much because, no matter what it is, people don't tend to want to hear you talk about your obsessions too much. Except a few friends who thought it was funny to call them Food Fighters to annoy me, I don't really think I hear too much negativity.

I don't play an instrument and I'm definitely not particularly physically skilled! I did try to learn guitar as a few years ago, and Foo Fighters definitely were one influence on that, but it didn't go well.

It's naturally very hard to say what their legacy's going to be. I think it's fair to say that despite their huge popularity they've not had such a huge impact on general popular culture, not in the same way a band such as Led Zeppelin or even Dave's 'other' band, Nirvana have. With that being said, I think the band will definitely still be one talked about in 50 years. They have too many great songs and stories to be forgotten.

# John

## Newcastle, UK
### ("Chris Shiflett" - Fu Fighters)

My tribute band's been together for since February 2012. Me and the original singer were in another band together. We were just a mixed covers band. Basically we did pop songs but tried to put a punk rock style edge on them.

I like the Foos but being in a Foo Fighters tribute band has made me a super fan of them. I like their music; I had a couple of their albums, and our singer did as well. We weren't aware of other Foo Fighters tributes at the time and thought that we could do it.

Our drummer does play in another band. He plays in a mixed rock covers band called 606 who are dotted around a similar area to where we live. They actually play more gigs than we do! It's good because we go for quality over quantity because tribute bands don't really suit your average bar gigs. But they do all the crowd pleasing stuff that will go down well anywhere.

When me and the singer finished the band we were in before – we just got bored with it – so we said to the other two lads that if they wanted to find people to replace us and carry on the band then they were free to. They didn't and me and Kev, who as the original singer, were just talking – we'd played together for years, since we were 15 or 16 -  and we wanted to continue doing something together. So we thought "What could we do next?". We have other friends who are in tribute bands and we thought "What about a tribute band?". It was something that we could get our teeth in to but it had to be a band that we both really, really liked and were passionate enough about to stick at. We threw around a few ideas; there was Metallica, Bon Jovi etc. But we thought about the original singer's voice and what would best suit him and what we both like. He was a good shouter which is brilliant for the Foo Fighters. We landed on that because it seemed like the logical choice. We both love the band and both our singing and playing styles suit what they do so we then advertised for the other two people that we need.

The main reason for the band, for me, is playing live. There's no better feeling than playing loud to a lot of people. I just love the sound of a dirty guitar through a big, big amp. It's hearing that tone that's unmistakable, the one that makes your neck hair stand up on end and gets your adrenaline going. I could say that I love music and that I love hearing what people do with music but it's just the sound of guitars more than anything else rather than music.

We do our best to dress like the Foos when we're on stage but we're humans and we're never going to change the aesthetics of the way we look other than maybe growing my hair. It's more about sounding like the band because if we sound like them we're going to get people more excited. It's about getting the feel and getting the ambiance of a Foo Fighters gig rather than just looking the part. It's more important that you sound like them and getting the songs right. We can do bits and bobs here and there. Like I said, the way we dress and getting the signature instruments. I know the bass player has Nate's bass, I've got Shiflett's signature Tele and the singer uses the drummer's Dave Grohl guitar from time to time. Other than getting the signature instruments, there's not really a lot we do to look the part.

It's quite hard for me not to be the person that I'm playing on stage. Chris Shiflett stands to the side and gets on with it really. But sometimes my own enthusiasm does take over and I will have the odd rock out. Like when you hit that middle section of *All My Life* you can't help yourself! Your head goes, your body moves, and if there's a drum riser I'll stand up there. There's also a few songs where, because we've got wireless systems, I get the chance to go out in to the crowd. Because the Foo Fighters are big enough to have the large runways and they have them so that they can go out in to the crowd to draw people in and allow everyone to experience what's going on. And us being able to do that allows us to do it in a similar way that the Foo Fighters do. So the bass player, yeah, he doesn't have to do much, either! Nate Mendel, he stands there. You get the odd head bob. The drummer's restricted by the fact that he's playing drums! But the singer, the singer definitely gets to act the part. He does the odd Dave Grohl sway when he's playing, the arm gestures, the shouts. He definitely has to more than any of the rest of us do. There are times when I have to try and rein myself in! 'cause I'm too excited with what we're doing, especially if it's a big show. You just get carried away! But I know that, especially for myself, if I'm seeing a band enjoying themselves, I'm going to enjoy myself even more. So it's not a bad thing that I'm into breaking character on stage.

We've got nearly 2,500 likes on Facebook and I know that a "like" is just a case of clicking a button but we do see a lot of the same faces at some of our gigs. We're on first name terms with a lot of the fans. In fact, we've been round to a few of their houses for drinks or barbecues, especially when England (football) matches are on. We go round and have a few drinks with them and hang out with their families. Yeah, we've got a good following. It's nice to see those people again and again because we know we're going to get a lot of participation off them.

When it comes to what we play on stage we have core songs in there that we know that people will want to hear but, no, we generally don't have the same set list. We will always mix it up. We were just having this debate for a big show that's coming up. We know what *has* to be there but we're playing a longer time slot so what do we fill the set out with?

There's like twenty odd songs that we could throw in but which ones are the right ones? Which ones will allow the set to flow? You've got to have your ebbs and flows and the songs have got to work with each other. You've got to think of guitar changeovers, too, because some of them are different tunings so which ones of those songs will take more time for you to do that? So the set list is never ever the same.

Crowds are insane! We love 'em! About four weeks ago, we were playing a gig at a venue called The Voyager in South Shields. It's just a bar that probably holds about three hundred people and there was probably about a hundred and fifty people there. There was a person right at the front. Adam played the first few notes of the song *Skin and Bones* and the person jumped up and, at the top of their voice, just screamed, "Fuck me! I can't believe they're playing this!". They turned to their mate, shook their head, and started jumping up and down because they were so excited to hear that particular song. As for other insanity from the crowds, there's a few photos from Bolt Fest, that we played earlier this year [2016], where I'm out front with the crowd and there's people with wide open mouths, just staring at me, which is weird because I'm not that good!

The biggest show we've ever played was probably Bolt Fest. There was around four thousand people there. The first year we played the audience was probably about half that. I don't really know; all I remember is the sea of faces. The first show we got with these organisers was completely out of the blue. I saw that they had a tribute festival and I'm cheeky so I'll ask for slots at gigs and at least get our name seen by someone who organises these events. They asked for the usual things; videos and recordings, so I sent those. And they invited us to play. That was in 2015. We did really well and got a good reaction from the crowd, so they asked us back to play this year which, to date, is the biggest show we've played. Off the back of that, we got the headlining slot at WV1 Fest which, when we've played it, will be the biggest one we've done.

When we first formed, it took a while to really get anything big going. We played a lot of support slots with other covers and tribute bands. So early on, because we were playing with tribute bands, it was maybe their crowds that weren't Foo Fighters crowds. For a long while there wasn't much going on. It was only when we got slots playing at the tribute weekends at the O2 Academy in Newcastle and a lot more people seeing us that our name was getting pushed to other corners of Facebook. That was actually how I found the Foo Family. One of them liked the band and then said, "Oh, have you seen this Foo Fighters Family?". So I joined! I go on to the group to advertise the gigs and help to spread the name along. But early on, it was really quite hard to get gigs. I'm not saying it's easy now. We still have to work to get gigs. We still have to make sure that we're good at what we're doing and I will still message other festivals to try and get us spots.

My main instrument is the Chris Shiflett Tele Deluxe, which is the most beautiful piece of kit that I've ever owned. I've never been a Tele player. I've always been a Les Paul player. But when I picked up the Tele; it's got the Humbucker pick-ups, which Chris uses, and the tone is just meaty and bright. Which is a weird combination. You don't get that very often on pick-ups. My back up guitars are two Les Paul customs. One's in Alpine White and the other is Silver Burst. I do have a jet black one, too, which is more of an ornament these days. Amp wise, I've got the Marshall AVT 4x12 cab with the AVT head which has the built in digital effects that I don't ever use. I just play through the clean channel on that and use all the effects through the floor pedal, which is a Boss ME80. It's an amazing piece of kit and it's the first floor pedal I've ever used in this style. I also use D'Addario gauge 11 strings, which are the same strings that Shiflett uses.

The bass player has the Nate Mendel Signature P Bass. The drummer has the Taylor Hawkins Signature Snare Drum, which is like an explosion when he hits it because he's a heavy hitter anyway. With the Taylor drum the sound is unmistakable and he's also got the guitar that Dave uses, the DG335. It's not the genuine article because they're about £7,000. This is a copy that he paid a few hundred pounds for which used to belong to the original singer. He got it made up and then upgraded the pick-ups and everything. The drummer bought it off him when the original singer left the band.

The copy guitars sound like complete shit when you first get them. You can put the same pick ups in that the real Foo Fighters use or you do your research online for the kind of pick ups you can buy that are going to get you a similar sound. Without the genuine article you'll never get the real sound. But you can do your tweaking with your pedals, your amps, and your tone dials to get it as close as possible to the actual sound. We've all now got the sound of the band nailed down.

What are the effects of the band? Probably friends made because of the band. I've met some good people and, like I said, some of them have become friends socially. I'd say that's going to be the most long lasting thing to take from the band. And hopefully giving people who have seen us moments where they feel euphoric about the Foo Fighters because, in that moment, that's exactly what they needed.

With the Foo Fighers, it's definitely giving people moments in their life that they're never going to forget. The Foos have done it for me. When I've seen them live and I've just been stood there in a moment, surrounded by 40,000 other people and not giving a flying fuck about who's around me. In that moment, it's me and the band. That's going to be their legacy; giving people moments in their life that are just great.

Some of my earliest music memories is watching Jools Holland's show, the Friday night show that he used to have on at about about 11pm. And I think I saw the Foo Fighters on there. That's one of my earliest memories of seeing them and going on to buy *The Colour and the Shape* album. Then I discovered that they'd got an album before that one so I went and bought that, too.

The band's my source of entertainment. Because I'm not a family man, I don't have kids and I'm not with anyone, so my band is kind of my life away from the usual nonsense. I look forward to the rehearsals [with my own band] because I get to play and be loud with people that I enjoy spending time with. Bar my family, they're probably the most important thing in my life. It's an escape and gives me a chance to forget about everything else. I'm appreciative of the Foos and what they've brought for me, my own band being a prime example.

I've only seem the Foos play live three times. The first time was Leeds festival about four years ago. I got on the barrier and was there for about two hours. Got within touching distance of Dave, Chris, and Nate. That was incredible, although painful. Stood on that barrier with fifty-odd thousand people behind you pushing forward, I had bruised ribs for about a fortnight afterwards. But it was totally worth it. I saw them when they did the closing ceremony at the Invictus Games down in London and, just last year [2015], I saw them at the Stadium of Light in Sunderland. I saw them just a couple of weeks before Dave broke his leg in Sweden. And to come back and finish the show in Sweden... What a guy. It's things like that which set them apart from every other artist on the planet. I can't think of anyone else doing that ever.

Sadly, I haven't met the band but it's on my bucket list. When we played one of our recent shows, there was this kid sitting on his Dad's shoulders and going mental to every song. This six year old kid, throwing the rock horns on top of his Dad's shoulders. I tried to get his Dad's attention because I wanted to try and get the kid on stage because he was genuinely going nuts and it was amazing to see. Afterwards, when we were clearing our gear off the stage and the crowd had dispersed, we heard this shout from behind. We turned around and it was the Dad and this little kid standing next to the barrier. He wanted to say that his son loved the show and wanted to say hello. So we all went down. It was me, Adam, and Ian, and we went over and started talking to the little lad. The kid was just absolutely beaming the whole time. You could tell that his Dad was properly proud of it, and rightly so because he's obviously raised the coolest little kid in the world. I just really, really enjoyed the fact that this kid loved every song we played. We got pictures of us and them and put them on our band's [Facebook] page. That's probably one of my favourite Foo Fighters related moments. I've also met a few of the Foo Fighters Family at the Sunderland gig. It was crazy because there's a lass [in the Family] who lives not too far from me so I arranged to meet up with her at the Sunderland gig. So I rang her and she took me to where all the other Family were hanging out. I was walking over and I didn't even have to introduce myself; they all knew who I was. Whether it's because of my band or whether it's because of the Family, you just feel settled in with those kinds of people straight away. It's just another example of how awesome Foos fans are. They're just great people and really welcoming.

Foo Fighters merchandise; I've got tshirts galore. Chris Shiflett's signature guitar. That's my main treasure. I've got a load of double F decals to put on our amps and guitar cases. We haven't got merchandise for our band but it is something that we've been talking about over the past couple of months. We want to try and get a few tshirts done up. I've got a few designs that I'd like to see on shirts but it's *what* to put on them because we've got to spend the money at the end of the day. I do think we'd be able to sell a few, especially to the North East members of the Foo Fighters Family. I think they'd definitely be up for buying some.

We were playing the weekend of the cancelled

Wembley shows. We couldn't get tickets for those shows so we booked a couple of our own. The venues were advertising our shows as "We can't get the real Foo Fighters but we've got these guys instead to help fill your Foo cravings". Which I wasn't complaining about; it was all good fun!

How to describe the Foo Fighters to someone who's never heard them before? I think I'd just say to them, "Listen to them. You'll love it! Seriously. Just. Listen. To. Them!". It would depend on which era of their career I was describing, too. If it was the early part, then I'd say that they're punk but with more of a rock edge. But now they're almost like heavy rock. As a genre, for me, they are just rock. Although I don't even think that their music can be pigeon-holed in to just that. I'd describe their songs as music that makes me feel something. If it makes someone feel something, whether it's happy or sad or whatever, then it's a good song. Most Foo Fighters songs do make me feel *something*. You hear the opening riff of *All My Life* and you can't help but go nuts. You wave your arms in the air when *Monkey Wrench* is on. You smile when *Big Me* starts. It's all music that makes me feel.

If I was going to give someone one of the band's songs to get them interested in the Foos then I'd probably base that choice on the kind of music that the person already likes. If it was someone who likes middle of the road rock music, I'd say listen to *Long*

*Road to Ruin, Big Me, Times Like These*. If it was someone who likes the heavier stuff, I'd say *The Pretender, Enough Space, Stacked Actors*. For someone who likes riff-based music, I'd say listen to the *Wasting Light* album. I can't just recommend one song, though if I had to, and it's going to seem like an obvious answer, but I'd probably say *Best of You*. My favourite song to play? I'd say *The Pretender* closely followed by *Bridge Burning*. My favourite song out and out? That's a question that I don't think I can answer!

My friends, family, and colleagues love that I'm so passionate about something. They say that when I talk about the band that I have a little light in my eyes. I'm always dead eager, as well, when I'm talking about the Foos, which can probably get a bit over the top sometimes. Everyone's really supportive both of my love of the Foos and of my tribute band.

The Foo Fighters lasting legacy on my life is providing moments at gigs when you can't help but smile. For me, they've provided some of my happiest gig-going memories. And, it might sound corny, but teaching me life lessons, too. Like the "Do unto others" attitude, which I think that we, as a band, try and emulate. And they've made me a better guitarist as well because their rhythm section is tight. Shiflett is a very good guitarist, probably better than I'll ever be.

In fifty years time, they'll be remembered as one of the greats, in the same way as Queen. Because, granted, there's never ever going to be another Freddie Mercury, Dave will always be one of the greatest front men who's ever lived. That'll span on through time, beyond fifty years as far as I'm concerned. They'll probably be remembered for writing some of the biggest ever rock songs again in the same way that Queen have.

The Fu Fighters are:

Daniel Gordon - Dave Grohl
Karl Cranswick – Taylor Hawkins
John Saunders – Chris Shifflet
Ian Craggs/Mark Pitchforth – Nate Mendel

# Jo
## Crawley, UK

I was out in Australia in 2000, visiting a friend, and this bloody rock station kept playing "Learn To Fly". And I was like, "What is this band?! This song's brilliant!". So I rang up my husband, who was my boyfriend at the time, and I said, "There's this band, called the Foo Fighters, and they've got this song out called *Learn To Fly*. Get me the album.". There was something about this song that just grabbed me and since then I've just become obsessed.

Everything. The Foos mean absolutely everything to me. When I have to do that crap called housework, I have them blaring. When I've had a really long day at work I put them on in the car on the way home, and I've got them blaring. When I'm upset I put them on, and I've got them blaring. There's just something about the music and the passion they have towards their fans as well is what it means to me. I will go to one of their concerts and I'm shaking with the adrenaline. Then the concert happens and I cry at the end. And then I turn round to my brother and say, "Well, when's the next concert?". They just leave you wanting more. Dave has you by the danglies. He knows how to play the crowd. It's just amazing and it's the passion that they put in to an album. They don't just record a load of songs in a week and then throw out another album. They think about what they're doing and how how they're going to do it. Like recording it in his [Dave's] garage or going all around America. I just find that fantastic. The passion they have for their music and for the fans, I have for the band.

I've seen the Foos at Hyde Park and the O2. I went to Wembley Stadium to see them. I went to Wembley Arena when they were NME's Godlike Genius for a year. I've seen them at Milton Keynes twice and I also got tickets for the Invictus Games. The Foo Fighters were the first concert that I took my daughter to. She was ten when we went and she was just blown away by it! My brother's been to the private gigs, the ones with two or three hundred people. Him and his girlfriend got on the guest list for one but couldn't get me a ticket. I was absolutely gutted and I didn't talk to him for two weeks afterwards! My boss doesn't get it. He's like, "Yeah, but you've seen them more than once. What's the point?".

Everyone I work with thinks I'm an absolute nutter because of my Foos obsession. My brother really likes the Foo Fighters but he's not obsessed like I am. My husband just shakes his head and rolls his eyes. He's used to it by now. My workmates just don't get it. And I don't get it that they don't get it! When I'm sat in the office, all by myself, because I'm a catering manager so I've got all the chefs and whatnot out in the kitchen, I just have the Foos blaring. Or I've got a concert playing on my iPad and they'll come in and say,

"What is the matter with you?". I don't know! I thought I was normal! The Foos have pulled me through the usual rubbish, you know. When I'm stressed, or sad, I just put their music on.

I've got one of Dave's guitar picks. It's my prized possession and no one's allowed to go near the picture frame that it's in. It was used at Reading the last time they were there and a friend of a friend was working there. After the Foos left he was one of the first on stage to clear up. And you can see where Dave used it, where it's all frayed at the edge. I've taken it to show a few friends but no one's allowed to touch it. They're not allowed to look at it, just in case it wears out! I've got all the usual t-shirts and the ones that say things like "Mentally dating Dave Grohl". My husband bought me that one for Christmas!

I'm always looking on eBay to see what there is, gold discs and stuff like that. I've got a picture that someone did of Dave Grohl. Really old picture actually; he's still got short hair. I do buy things like that and put it away or very quietly put it up somewhere in the house. The husband comes home from work and he's like, "More shit...". My obsession is getting worse!

Back in 2003, I was going to LA; we went to Australia that way. And I'm kicking myself now because I didn't go and look for the studio. 'Cause I'd have gone and looked for it and stood there waiting for them to turn up! They'd probably have been somewhere else in the world but I'd just be stood there, waiting them! But I think what they do is absolutely fantastic and I think more bands should be like that with doing everything themselves and shouldn't be controlled by these big record companies.

They've kept me going through all the shit. It's just something about the music, it's just... wow. It just hits a nerve. I've been through depression and all stuff like that and I just put the Foos on and sit there and I'm happy again.

How would I describe the band? Fucking awesome! They're the whole package. Their music, their attitudes, the way they make records. Just how different they are. I could sit and watch their videos 'til the cows come home. You know, they don't take themselves too seriously and they enjoy doing what they're doing. They go off and do different projects and then they come back again. There you go; they're the whole package!

*Times Like These* is the song I'd recommend anyone listens to first. It's just the best song. It's awesome and I love it. When they do it slow, when they do fast... It's the song of theirs that I'd give anyone. It's my absolute favourite song.

I don't play an instrument but my daughter has started playing guitar and it's purely because of the Foo Fighters. She's eleven and a half and she's just changed guitar teacher. One of the first songs her new teacher taught her was *My Hero*. Whenever she goes for a lesson, that's the song they warm up to. I'm so proud!

You know the album cover where Dave has the two F's on his neck? I have the exact same tattoo on my shoulder. I'm really proud of this tattoo. I'm not embarrassed by it all and I don't mind showing it off. Not one person who doesn't like the Foo Fighters has turned round and said, "You absolute idiot. You shouldn't have done that." They've all gone, "Oh my god, wow!".

They knew how to rock and the energy in their concerts is insane. Some groups you go and see are just going through the motions. But the Foo Fighters aren't. They love it as much as the fans. It's them live and the appreciation that they have for the fans as well. They've always got time for their fans. The band don't brush the fans off and tell them to do one. Which is lovely, and they show as much respect as we show back to them. That's going to be their legacy.

# Fooz Fighters
## California, USA

The band was formed in 2014 and some members have been playing together for over twenty years. Prior to forming Fooz Fighters, guitarist Brent played in a successful Stone Temple Pilots tribute band called Vasoline which disbanded when the lead singer quit. Brent then decided to launch another tribute project and Foo Fighters kept sticking out due to their huge catalogue of hits and the fact that they were from the West Coast and there seemed to be few other quality Foo Fighters tribute bands existing. The project came together when Nicky Rich agreed to join the band as "Dave Grohl".

We wanted a band with a wide audience appeal and one that is currently relevant. As mentioned above they have a huge catalogue of hits and are truly an "Arena" rock act with so many sing a long hits make it the perfect tribute band. Their music has spanned 3 decades and they continue to tour and release new music that is arguably their best material ever. We knew that if we found the right lead singer that looked and sounded like Dave Grohl we would be successful.

For us, it's all about the live performance seeing the crowd sing along and go crazy and knowing that we have touched people in a positive way. For our larger shows we do meet and greets and so many people tell us how we made their day and can't wait to see us again. There are so many problems in the world and it makes us feel so good to know that somehow for 90 minutes we can take people to a different place away from the everyday problems.

Well, as you know Foo Fighters are all about Dave Grohl and maybe Taylor Hawkins but to a lesser degree so having a lead singer that looks like Dave is very important if you want to really give people the Foo Fighters experience. We are very fortunate to have Nicky Rich who not only looks like Dave but nails his vocals and high energy stage presence. Other than Taylor Hawkins the rest of the band members of Foo Fighters (Pat, Chris and Nate) are pretty nondescript but yes we are constantly working on our look and tweaking it to be the best we can. Having said this just looking like the band does you no good unless you actually sound like the band. We are very extremely detailed in our approach to play these songs note for note right down to every nuance. The biggest compliments we receive are those related to how much we sound like the Foo Fighters.

Yes, stage persona is all part of being the best tribute band you can be so each of us watch a ton of video to make sure we are as closely resembling the members as possible. People pay money to see our shows so we owe it to our fans to be the best we can be.

We've built quite a following over the past 18

months starting with playing small bars and clubs to now headlining major concert venues like House of Blues, festivals and casinos. Our fans are great and we see many of the same faces at our shows. The best part is we see families at our shows so the ages can range from teens to older adults and everything in between.

We've had several shows where people jump up on stage. We've seen mosh pits with fans body slamming each other and we always have fans dancing and singing along.

On 24th September 2015, the Foo Fighters played a sold out show at San Diego Cricket Wireless Amphitheater. Half way through the song Arlandria, Dave Grohl noticed a crazy fan dancing wildly in the front row. He proceeded to pull him up on stage where the videos of "Happy Feet Steve" went viral on social media. Several months later at a Fooz Fighters show at House of Blues in San Diego we were able to bring Happy Feet Steve up on stage with us to recreate the moment. The crowd loved it.

Our biggest show was probably the first time we played House of Blues in San Diego. We were given the opportunity by the Red Not Chili Peppers, the best RHCP tribute band in the World to open for them and several other established tribute bands. The place was packed wall to wall and what really surprised us was how many people in the crowd were there to see us. We knew right away that we could really build this project into something special.

We receive a ton of fan mail mostly people asking us when we are playing next or requesting that we travel to other states and countries. It's very humbling and we always to our best to get back to people as soon as possible. It's not uncommon after our shows for fans to ask for our used guitar picks, drum sticks, etc.

Foo Fighters fans are the best in the world. We have received nothing but positive feedback all along the way and are constantly blown away by their loyalty to all things Foo Fighters. It's like one big happy family. We are thankful to be part of that.

In most cases we use the same instruments as the Foo Fighters. Brent plays a Fender Custom Chris Shiflett telecaster, of course, Nicky plays a Dave Grohl Custom 335 model in Pelham blue.

We absolutely do feel like we provide some kind of relief when the Foos are on a break. When we started this project the Foo Fighters had just announced their world tour but now that they are taking a break we find that people really miss seeing them and come to our shows to celebrate the music of the Foo Fighters.

Our goal is to be the best we can be and if we stay focused on that goal everything else will take care of itself. So far this has worked well for us we are headlining major venues, concert halls, festivals and casinos and playing to packed crowds. We have a tour of the east coast planned for early next year with stops in New York, Philadelphia and New Jersey.

I think it helps that we're in California (where the Foo Fighters are based) but there are Foo fans everywhere in the world. We get messages from Mexico, Latin America, Italy and the UK to play shows.

We have not had any legal issues so far. We have created our own logo so as not to infringe on any patent rights. My advice to anyone thinking about starting a tribute band is to do your own branding. Create something unique that salutes the band but gives it your own personal spin.

If we had a message for up and coming artists, it would be Practice, Practice, Practice! As Dave Grohl says "work at your craft".

Fooz Fighters are from San Diego, CA and feature:
Nicky Rich – Lead Singer
Brent Wright – Guitar
**Alan Sosa** – Guitar
Noel Conklin – Bass
Mario Garduno – Drums

# Kelly
## Devon, UK
### (Admin for Foo Family UK)

My husband is a huge Nirvana fan and he followed the Foos from there. Sixteen years ago I met my husband and when we got together I started listening to different music as we were both discovering what each other liked, and I really did like the Foos

Oh my, I can't remember what the first song I heard was! The first album of theirs that I bought was the self-titled one as it's always best to start at the beginning. I then went from there.

The band means a lot to me, not only have I met some of my best friends via the band but I've also had some amazing experiences because of it.

I've seen the Foos play several times, including 2005 and 2007 at Birmingham, the Wembley 2008 show, Milton Keynes Bowl in 2011 and 2015, and Reading Festival 2012. I got to see them when they returned to the stage with Dave's broken leg at their 20th anniversary show in Washington in 2015. In 2013, I saw the Sound City Players in London. I was also lucky enough to receive a *Sound City* tape in the post when the film was being promoted, which Dave then signed for me at the Sound City Players gig.

In 2014, we set up a Kickstarter to raise awareness of ticket touting by having a fan funded Foo Fighters show in Birmingham, England. The campaign hit its £150,000 in just under a week and received national and international attention. While it didn't go any further than the Kickstarter, it was a great experience.

We have our own range of merchandise that we sell via Redbubble. Every year we choose a charity and all of the proceeds from the Foo Fam's merchandise go to that charity. Over the years we've supported Mind, Marie Curie, and The Alzheimer's Society.

I started a Facebook group six years ago, it's gone from strength to strength to the point where Facebook just couldn't cope with what we wanted to do so we created the website. The website is used to collect fans stories of seeing, and meeting, the band.

I'd describe the band as honest, credible, transparent rock – something that everybody can relate to. *Best of You* would be the one song that I'd give to someone who was trying to get in to the band.

My friends and family have learned to love the band. They had no choice! Even my 87 year old Nan tells me, "Kelly, I've seen that Foo Fighting man on the telly box last night", bless her.

I used to get negative reactions when I talked about the band. Now I very rarely bring them up but if they are mentioned I jump straight in.

I have some tattoos that are Foo related but not obviously so. I have feathers on my ankle representing Dave's feathers on is arms and I have a butterfly on my back to remember our very special trip to the 20<sup>th</sup> anniversary show in Washington DC in 2015.

# Sarah
## Texas, USA

Music has always been my 'sanctuary'. I have always turned to music whenever I need to retreat from the world. When I have things going on in my life that I don't want to think about, I escape things by putting on some music and losing myself in it. I remember being 6 or 7 years old and listening to my uncle's David Bowie albums and being absolutely enthralled. I asked for a couple of Bowie albums as my Christmas presents and I have been a rock fan ever since. There is something about music that heals something in me. Without music I don't think I would be the same person I am today. Music has shaped me and my life.

How did I get into Foo Fighters? Like many people I was a Nirvana fan and so when Dave formed Foo Fighters I was interested in listening to his new project. I heard a few tracks on the radio but I didn't really get into Foo Fighters until a few years later when a girl I was working with, who was a big fan, got me to listen to the albums and that was it....I was hooked.

The Foos music is fun, loud, and just fucking rock and roll (as Dave is so fond of telling us!). It's really hard to pick one song that I'd give to someone who didn't know Foo Fighters but I'd probably go with *The Pretender* because it kind of sums up the band. It has the typical loud/quiet format that I feel gives the band its 'sound' and also Dave's growling, half screamed vocals that are just so much of the character of the songs. The lyrics, "What if I say I'm not like the others", are all about breaking free from oppression and tyranny. Whilst Foo are not a political band this track was written about the political unrest in the USA at the time but the lyrics could equally relate to Dave wanted to break free from the 'Ex drummer of Nirvana' label and the backlash he got from some quarters when he started Foo Fighters after Kurt's death. It also connects to me on a personal level relating to a controlling relationship I was in and eventually breaking free of that.

And that is kind of something I love about Dave – his lyrics are quite often open to interpretation, which causes a lot of debate in the fan groups. But everyone has their own personal take on what the lyrics mean, and how they relate to them. Which makes for a greater connection to the band, and to hear a song you have a very personal connection to live can be completely overwhelming. I've seen people with tears rolling down their faces at Foo shows, totally caught up in the music, caught up in the emotion of what that song means to them. I've been there myself crying to *These Days* at a show a few weeks after I lost my cat – she died in my arms, closed her eyes and her heart stopped beating – so when they played that song with those lyrics I just felt the emotions all over again.

I think the Foos popularity, especially after 2008, was based around their anthems and their sound, they became a 'stadium band'. Certainly I feel that was the case in the UK especially after the Wembley shows. Their songs are very catchy and very sing-a-long. They're not complicated songs at all. You could put the Foo Fighters on the bill of any festival anywhere in the world and people would stop and listen. They might not know all the songs but they'd know more than a couple. Of course, there are some people who say that they hate the Foo Fighters. But I don't think that anyone would leave just because they were on the stage. I think that the band appeal to such a wide audience that yes, you could say, in that respect, that they are the "last great rock band". And I think a lot of it is down to their personalities. They don't take themselves too seriously, they have fun and they totally engage the audience. It's a show without being showy – they do not need huge stage sets or a cast of thousand dancers to capture the audience's attention. The Glastonbury show in 2017 absolutely defines that sentiment. And that sets them apart from other groups, I think, that and the fact that they are just a group of 'ordinary' guys who happen to be able to make a living by doing something they love.

The band members don't live in ivory towers. They live ordinary lives. They take their kids to school. They go shopping in the supermarket. They're just ordinary people doing ordinary things and I think that's what people love about them. They're not pretentious in any way, shape, or form. Yes, they make a very good living but they don't shove that down people's throats. It's all about making music that they love, making music that people love, and it's about the fans. They get it because the band are big music fans themselves and they know what it's like to be in love with a band. You only have to look at the Foo members outside of the band to realise just how big of music fans they are. You'll see Dave at shows, and not necessarily at the side of the stage but actually out in the crowd. They still get star struck when they meet their music heroes, Dave will still 'fanboy out' and get over excited at the musicians he meets. Chris has his 'Walking The Floor' podcast which showcases all kinds of different music and musicians. Taylor has an encyclopedic knowledge of 70's/80's rock and gets excited to visit studios where classic rock albums were made. The guys are music lovers just like their fans.

A large proportion of the fan base are about the same age as the band. We've grown up with the band over the last 20 years or so, our lives are in the same cycle as the band. They're married and have kids, as have we. And one of the great things is that the fans bring their kids to Foo shows. Even though Dave swears like a trooper when he's on stage, the parents will still bring their kids because they want them to experience this band. It's like a family thing now, a true Foo family where you can take your kids along and share the experience.

I didn't really get involved in the Foo Family, as the fan base is called, until 2015. I moved to Canada in 2011 and missed the *Wasting Light* tour. But then I moved down to the USA in 2014 so I was around for the *Sonic Highways* tour. I went to a few shows on my own. I get to the venue really early as I like to try and get to the front on the rail, and just ended up chatting to people in the line. People were very friendly. We all looked out for each other by holding places in line whilst we took turns going to get food or use the restrooms, and we just had fun swapping stories and chilling out. We kept in touch on Facebook but it wasn't until 2016 when I went to several Chevy Metal shows [one of Taylor's side projects] that I really got involved with the Foo community. I was already a member of the Foo postboard, the discussion forum linked to the official Foos website, but I also became involved with a number of Facebook groups including the Taylor Hawkins Fan Page, where I am now a page admin.

On the whole, the fan groups are fun and, considering how big the band is, the fan groups are actually quite small – I know a lot of people in the USA groups as we all tend to meet up at shows and other events. There is more activity during an album/tour cycle where people join/come back to the groups but during the down times it is usually just a smaller core of people. The groups have a big tradition of sending out 'Foo Mail' between members; this might be something as simple as a notecard or could be Foo related gifts, and it is always a really nice surprise to get a parcel with 'Foo Mail' written across it. Fan merchandise is quite a big thing in the fan community where people make Foo based items to send out to people; we have some very creative people in the fan groups. I have had quite a lot of fan merchandise made to send out including wristbands, postcards, guitar picks, candles, chocolate coins, badges and coasters which I send out as parcels to people I have spent time with at shows, or people who are going through a tough time and need a boost.

I did a lot of fan merchandise for Chevy Metal in 2016 which I managed to get to the band – I have seen photos of Taylor and Dave wearing the wristbands I made which is fantastic – and I also gave Dave one of my FF wristbands last year when I bumped into him at the CalJam festival.

There are a lot of collectors within the fan group and they collect everything related to the band; records, posters, stickers, badges, anything and everything! I have a good sized collection which I keep in my 'Foo Room' but I still have a load of posters I haven't gotten around to getting framed and a load of smaller items which I just don't have the space to display. That doesn't stop me buying more stuff as I find it or as the band releases more items via their online store! It's amazing to see the collections some fans have. I love to see their photos of their posters, collectables and most of all their photos of themselves with the band. I love that people get that meet the boys and have a photo as a memory of that special time.

Meeting the band is obviously what most fans want to do because they just want to express to them [the band] how much they mean to them. The band have the reputation of being very generous with fans, taking time to sign stuff, chatting and taking photos. In the close knit Foo community there is very little jealousy. Everybody shares the love. I went to Hotel Saint Cecilia – the small hotel in Austin where FF stayed and recorded *Saint Cecilia.* I stayed there for a couple of nights and everyone was just so excited for me rather than being jealous or judgmental or saying what a groupie I was. They just wanted to see photos of the hotel and hear about what it was like. Everyone shares in the experience. We share the experience of being a fan with each other.

My friends and family think I'm a crazy fangirl but they love it as well because they know that I've made so many friends through being a fan. If I go to a show, I will never be on my own even if I physically went on my own because there will always be someone there that I know. They do think I'm crazy for standing outside, in all weathers in a line, sometimes for fourteen hours, waiting for the doors to open. What motivates me to do that? To get on the rail! I know it's not the best place acoustically to stand, but you can interact with the band because they're very interactive on stage. The band, especially Dave, recognise people who've been to multiple shows. He'll talk to them so you get that interaction when you're at the front. It's part of the fun of being at a show.

I don't really get negative reactions to being a fan. People either know the band and like them or they don't know who the band are at all. I've never had anyone say, "Oh my God, they're fucking awful.". A lot of the time the reaction you do get, I've found, is that you get people who say, "Oh, wasn't he the guy who was in Nirvana?". Or, "I don't really like their music but Dave Grohl is cool." Even if you're not a Foo fan, pretty much everyone in the world knows who Dave Grohl is. But outside of the Foo community, people wouldn't necessarily know the names of everyone else. Taylor, they may know, but not the rest of the guys. They don't put themselves out there like other bands do and there's not much gossip or scandal around them. I think that's why they're popular in our community as well is because they don't have that scandal attached. They don't have that horrible demeanour about them where they're nasty to their fans or the press. They're just ordinary guys. You can imagine going down the pub with the band and having a really good time, no pretentious 'I'm a rockstar' shit, just a few drinks and lots of laughter.

Music, and musical diversity, is important to the band so outside of Foo Fighters they all have their own projects. If you're not very active in the Foo community, you wouldn't particularly know about the side projects because they don't really advertise them and you don't see a load of adverts saying, "Taylor Hawkins of Foo Fighters", or "Lieutenant, featuring Nate Mendel of Foo Fighters". But the fan base is so loyal that the side projects become an extension of Foo Fighters. And because they do quite a long hiatus between album and tour cycles, it's a way for us fans to keep together and meet up and to keep the excitement going of what the band's going to do next going. Chevy Metal, for example, was put together just as a fun party band to keep Taylor active and it's grown in to its own thing. Taylor's other side band, Taylor Hawkins and the Coattail Riders, was absolutely called that because he was riding on the Foo Fighters coattails! The side projects are a big part of the Foo community and everyone supports them. Plus it's great to see the individual members having fun outside of Foo and being the front men for a change.

Bands that play as support for Foo Fighters instantly become part of the fan community and fans will support them in their own right by buying tickets to their shows after their tour with Foo Fighters is over. It is the same thing when one of the Foos play with another band or recommend their music, the Foo fans will take the time to listen and maybe discover a new band to enjoy. I have ended up listening to and going to see bands just because of Foo Fighters, which I know the boys would be thrilled about. They want people to love music as much as they do.

I have so many special stories relating to the band. For me it's been more than meeting the band; I've met Dave, Taylor, Chris and Pat, and more about friendships made through following the band. It's more the fun we have when we're standing outside together for hours on end, just having a laugh, sharing stories, sharing the excitement at shows, and the little gifts and notes. They're the special stories, really. The fans look after and care about each other – it may have been the love of Foo Fighters that brought us together but it is the friendships that we have made that keep us together. Some of the people I have met through Foo Fighters are people I will be friends with for the rest of my life.

The band's lasting legacy on my life takes me back to the same things; friendship and love. Just being part of the soundtrack to my life, giving me hope and getting me through some dark times. Which is why *Times Like These* will always be one of my favourite Foo Fighters tracks because the message of that track sums up everything the band stands for in my life...

# Sue

## Cardiff, Wales

### (Admin for **www.foofightersuk.com**)

How did I discover them? I'd sort of seen them on Kerrang TV. It wasn't until Live Earth [2007] where they played a little set that I really noticed them. I saw *Everlong* for the first time where he [Dave] does the first bit acoustically by himself. And then the rest of the band came out and I was like, "Wow! Why haven't I taken more notice of this band before?". And that's when I properly discovered them.

The first song of theirs that I think I heard was *Learn to Fly*. The video was on and I thought that it was extremely funny and loved that they were playing all these different characters. I love their sense of humour!

The first album that came out after I'd gotten to like them was *Echoes, Silence, Patience, and Grace*, although *One By One* was the one that I got in to first.

What does the band mean to me? Happiness. Relativity because they just seem to be relevant to me. They're also true and real. There's no falseness. They're doing it because they want to and not because it's what they think that people want to hear. They stay true to themselves.

The first gig of theirs that I saw was Milton Keynes Bowl in 2011. Second time was Reading 2012. I saw them at the House of Vans when they played as The

Holy Shits [2014]. Invictus Games [2014]. If you can count it, I saw the Sound City Players [2013]. Lastly, there was Milton Keynes [2015].

As for a special story, I guess that it would be meeting Dave at the cinema in Leicester Square at the première of *Sound City*. Along with one of my friends, I met him half way through the film at the bar and got at least ten minutes of him all to ourselves. I managed to act like a dumbstruck teenager. All the questions that I'd ever wanted to ask him went out of my head and I just stood there looking at him. It was like watching it happen to someone else; it was surreal. We started talking to him and I started acting like a goldfish. We talked to him about the film and the girl I was with, Amy, had her photo taken with him. And then I asked him if I could have a photo with him and he said, "Sure". He put his arm round me and I thought, "Oh my God! He's put his arm round me, I better put my arm round him.". So I had my photo taken and said, "Thanks.". Around about then some other fans approached him and he was posing for photos with them and talking to them. This guy gave Dave a black marker and asked him to draw on his arm. Dave asked him if he was sure and the guy replied that he was. So he drew a self portrait on this guy's arm. While he's stood there doing that, I thought, "Oh my God. I want him to write on *me*.". The guy threw me his marker and I asked Dave if he would add to my Foo Fighters tattoo. When I showed it to him, he said, "Oh my God, I've got one like that!". And I said, rather stupidly, "Yeah, I know...". He asked me if I was sure that I wanted him to write on me and I said that I was. So he signed his name under my tattoo and I thanked him. Then me and my friend walked around around the corner, looked at each other and screamed, as if to say, "Oh my God! Has that just happened?!". We went back down in to the auditorium and tried to watch the rest of the film but, after that, it was really hard to concentrate. All the people behind us were telling us to shut up because the whole row of us had managed to meet him and we were talking excitedly about it.

It was about three days after I met Dave that I got his autograph tattooed on me because we were in London the next day for the Sound City Players gig. So I tried not to wear anything on it, rolled up my sleeve, and got one of my friends to go back over it with a pen. We did go around Kings Cross to try and find a tattooist to do it but we didn't have any luck. Most of them were fully booked and the earliest appointment I could get would have been after I'd got home. So I had it tattooed three days later when I got back to Wales. Dave's signature did pretty well considering that it was in permanent marker. The tattooist didn't want to tattoo over it and had to trace it before washing it off, which was pretty horrible! I hated him washing it off but because it was a permanent marker, he didn't want that ink getting in to my skin.

As for unofficial merchandise, there's the Foo Fam tshirt and the wristbands that I had made for the Foo Family. I came up with the design for them and Dave actually got given one by an American Fam member. He put it on and wore it for a couple of tracks when he played the Record Store Day gig [April 2015]. I was so chuffed by that! Those wristbands mean a lot to me because it was one that I'd designed. I designed it with the rock hand and the infinity symbol [featured on *Sonic* Highways artwork] but I had them printed as inlays as the writing was rubbing off the old ones. I wanted those ones to be a bit more durable. I kept six of the ones that I designed for the Birmingham gig that didn't happen, ready to give to the band. I'm pretty sure that we had tshirts for them as well and, even though the gig didn't happen, you don't know what the future's going to hold. I'm not sure what other Foo Fam merchandise there's going to be but I know that Taylor and Rami have met Foo Fam wearing the Foo Fam tshirts.

One other piece that I have is one that a friend made for me. I knew someone who worked in a tshirt shop and he had a cut out of Dave's silhouette that he had that printed on one of my tshirts for me.

I joined the Foo Fam about six months after it was started. I wasn't in the Foo Fam from the very beginning but I was there from the first year. When I joined, I think there was about three hundred members and there's about fifteen thousand now. I think it was Kelly who first used the term "Foo Family" because, before that, the group had another name. I've never seen fans like Foo Fighters fans before. This is the only band I've seen where the fans are like this. When I went to my first Foo Fighters show I was surrounded by all these people who I thought were as crazy a Foo Fighters fan as I was. But when I tried to engage them, I found that they weren't. So when I got home, I looked at Facebook, and found the Foo Fam. Finding that group felt like coming home. All of a sudden I didn't feel like I was the only crazy Foo Fighters fan out there! The fans have made me feel less alone. It's nice to be able to be with people who "get it", and who understand your passion and to be able to have conversations with them about it. You don't feel like you have to explain yourself or give reasons why you like the band. Because they already know it and they feel the same way that you do.

Back in 2014, I was part of a very small team who ran a Kickstarter to get the Foos to play Birmingham. The Kickstarter was aimed at getting attention for the secondary ticket market, which the Foos had mentioned in the *Sonic Highways* TV series. We, as well as the band, had seen it happen so many times; people had tried to buy tickets to a show, any show, and been locked out because the secondary ticket sellers were hoovering them all up.

The Kickstarter was Kelly's idea but it was great to be a part of something so big. We spammed the Hell out of the ticket tout and music pages, trying to get attention for the Kickstarter. We had a little group on Facebook for sharing ideas and information on how to get the news out there. It was amazing how much attention that Kickstarter got and we easily hit the target of £150,000. The whole thing was definitely a great experience, especially seeing how excited people got about it.

How would I describe the band to someone who'd never heard them before. I can't say that they're a good old fashioned rock and roll band because they're more than that. I'd say that they're a rock band with a good sense of humour and who keep it real.

If it was someone who was in to more heavier stuff, I'd give them *White Limo* to listen to as an intro to the band. But if it was someone who was in to lesser-rocky type music it would probably be *Learn to Fly* because it's one of their more run-of-the-mill songs that someone who wasn't in to rock music could quite happily listen and relate to.

My immediate family have had no choice but to love the Foo Fighters because I've always played them and the kids have grown up listening to them. My Mum thinks they're great because they make me happy. My other, less-immediate family, know how much that I love them so they're quite happy about it but some of them think that I'm a complete and utter nut! They think that I'm a totally, full on fan but then I remind them that there are people out there who are even bigger fans than I am! My husband is encouraging and supportive and even he got sucked in to being a fan in the end, to the point of having the double F's tattooed on his arm!

The first tattoo I had; I always knew I wanted one but I couldn't decide what. So I didn't have my first tattoo until I was thirty nine and that was the Foo Fighters F's on my arm. A lot of my friends thought that I was bonkers and stupid. They were saying, "Oh, what if the band split up?" Or "What happens if Dave turns out to be a serial killer? What would you do then?". And I said that it didn't matter because it's what the band means to me now and the tattoo will always be a reminder of what they mean to me. That tattoo is now the one that Dave added his signature to. It was supposed to be a fireball in the shape of a guitar with the Fs in the middle. Then I had a treble clef with musical notes wrapped around it. And then Dave's signature underneath. At the same time that I had his signature tattooed, I had *All My Life* added to the top of it.

The band's legacy on my life will be that photo of Dave and me. It's always going to be my profile picture on Facebook. The Foo Family website will always be a part of my life, too. Kelly created it but she passed it on to us. When we took it over, we gave it a new design. My daughter designed the banner on the front page and I'm generally in charge of the upkeep of it. I guess that's the band's lasting legacy on me.

I think the band's legacy in fifty years time will be the way they've brought fans together from all over the world. I also think it's the way that Dave has reached out to so many other bands and singers and songwriters and shown how versatile he is. He's someone who's managed to play with all of his childhood heroes and everyone seems to love the Foos. And hopefully Dave inspired another generation of rock musicians.

# Poppy
## Cholsey, UK

It was through my love of Nirvana that I first discovered Dave Grohl. I was devastated by the death of Kurt Cobain and when Foo Fighters formed it was a natural part of the healing process and lessened the deep shock and feeling of loss at the end of Nirvana, a band that will be forever part of history. I've been a fan of the Foos since the beginning.

*This Is A Call* is the first song of theirs that I remember hearing. I was hooked straight away on the sound of Foo Fighters and knew I would be a lifelong fan. Their self titled album in 1996 was one of my first ever albums, bought on the same day as my first owned copy of Nevermind. I was 13.

For me, music is one of the greatest things in life, and no matter how broken I may be feeling, the Foo Fighters music speaks to my soul, helping me release that inner turmoil. If I'm feeling happy, that feeling is intensified by their music until I'm jumping around like an excited teenager. If I'm angry, I will sing along until that anger dissipates completely. I may age in life but their music continues to ignite my inner child.

2002 Reading festival was my first ever big festival and the highlight was seeing Foo Fighters live. It cemented my love for them as not only a band with great music but a band whose live performance was unforgettable. To17-year-old me it was life changing with thousands of people from different walks of life all connected by one band, speaking to each person in a different but equally powerful way. This was the beginning of my love of festivals and live music.

One of my best friends as a teenager shared my love of all things grunge, rock, and alternative music. We spent many sunny summer afternoons listening to music including the Foo Fighters and attempting to play along ourselves. While my friend was extremely musically talented I was only match them with my unrelenting enthusiasm.

Years ago I had a lot of band merchandise especially badges, t-shirts and bags. But, as the kids have come along, my collections, and money to add to my collections, have dwindled. One of my few guilty pleasures is buying music and I'm a sucker when limited edition albums are released. I'm in the beginning stages of creating merchandise for a community group I'm involved in and music merchandise will be what I use as inspiration as its really the only kind, along with films, that I've ever brought.

Music in general inspires me to live a better life. It has the power to change your emotions and, in turn, the way you deal with your circumstances in life. Foo Fighters are no exception to this. The impact that music can bring into your life can never be underestimated. When you are at your lowest it has the ability to stop you feeling like the only person in the world feeling that way, connecting you with the importance of being alive. When you are upbeat it connects you to those feelings, amplifying and celebrating those moments of happiness. Music is more powerful than any anti-depressant that can be prescribed.

The fact that over twenty years later myself and millions of others are still listening to Foo Fighters speaks volumes to the talent of the band. Great music that still speaks to me at so many levels, different levels to those lazy summer days, deeper levels as I've grown. I love their music as much as I always have and I'm sure that love will never die.

When my daughter was a baby I was in a very violent relationship and listening to Foo Fighters as well as other bands helped when it came to empowering me to leave the situation I was in. The song *Best of You* especially spoke deeply to me at the time, but in general the words of each song has the ability to reach into a certain part of my life. *One by One* was another song that hit many nerves for me, as well as *Times Like These*. I think Foo Fighters do not receive the credit they deserve for their song writing abilities. While I'm aware that some of the early music had less depth, it still spoke to the teenage me on many levels.

A brilliant rock band whose music combines rock with a hint of grunge, pop and punk in the mix is how I'd describe them alone with being one of the most talented groups of musicians on the planet.

That's a hard one, picking one song that you'd give to someone. *Best of You* is a song that really spoke to me at a particularly hard time in life, so I suppose I would begin with that, although songs such as *Everlong* with their lyrics and videos would also be great ones to share with others. I think there is not one song I don't like so I think it would depend on the person I was showing them too. I would also tell people of the collaborations that Dave is involved in such as working with Tenacious D. I love his sense of humour and seeing him appear in other bands videos.

Most of my friends and family do not share my love of music although both my brothers are fans. It's very hard when you are surrounded with people who have a very different taste in music, but in my opinion it's their loss.

The reaction I normally receive from those around me is "Who?". Which always frustrates me. The Foos normally have a bit of recognition if I mention Nirvana but that is only minimal. Unfortunately, in my village alternative people are few and far between and it's rare I can have a conversation on music that doesn't involve the words "how can you listen to that?".

My passion for music is huge, my talent for playing music is not. This is something I find hard as I would love to have the talent on the guitar that Dave has. I've been inspired to play by so many musicians but unless I meet the Devil and sell my soul for the talents I don't believe I will every come close to the greats.

Great music has a never-ending legacy and Foo Fighters write and perform great music that will never lose its impact on those who listen. For every generation, there will be bands who have been inspired by those before them, the Foo Fighters have inspired others since the beginning and will continue to inspire long after they are gone.

# Laurel
## Texas, USA

I followed Dave over from Nirvana. I was in my late teens and into my early twenties when Nirvana broke. Pretty much the perfect age for their fan base. Along with most of their fans, the first time I heard the band was when the Smells Like Teen Spirit video came on MTV. I immediately went out and bought the *Nevermind* cassette tape. Over the next few months, I really got into the band; they became one of my absolute favourites. I bought all their tapes and cassingles (cassette singles - remember those?) and every magazine that even mentioned Nirvana. I was there when Kurt and Courtney had Frances Bean and they had feuds with other bands like Guns n' Roses, and watched all their appearances on the MTV Video Music Awards - I ate every bit of it up gleefully.

Dave was there in the background the whole time. He wasn't as dramatic as Kurt and Courtney, but he was a great drummer, and pretty cute. And then Kurt died. And it all ended.

But not for Dave. He made a comeback with the Foo Fighters. Kurt's death had silenced an entire band, and he could have given up and gotten into some other line of work. In fact, I remember Dave saying in an interview from his Nirvana days that he wasn't going to be like the Scorpions and still be playing music in his 40s and 50s, that he was going to do something else with his life. So when he came back with a new band, I was a bit surprised but very delighted to see his cute face on my TV again.

The Foos were just full of surprises! Dave wasn't playing the drums! Not only could he play guitar, but he could also sing lead! I knew Dave could sing great backup because we saw him doing that in Nirvana (especially the *Unplugged* special), but I had no idea he could sing lead so well. I was so proud of him! Not only had he come back from a terrible tragedy, but Dave was multi-talented musically. I had no idea!

*I'll Stick Around* was the first song that I remember hearing. I wasn't sure who Dave was singing to, if he was supposed to be singing to anyone from his own perspective, but I really liked the defiant lyrics. The declaration of "I don't owe you anything!" - I could really relate to that. The video was great too. I had no idea for years that the big tentacle ball was supposed to be Courtney Love. There was such a great personal story behind everything surrounding the song. It was Dave's way of saying that he had a right to go on with his life, and no one had a right to stop him or tell him how to do it. He was and continues to be his own person with his own talents.

I haven't seen them live yet, but I'm going to see them play in Dallas, Texas in 2018! I can't wait! It's a night I have been waiting for for a very long time.

The only real merchandise that I have are CDs and cassettes. I can't really remember having seen their merchandise in stores very much. The items they sell on their web store are great, but kind of expensive. So I don't have much.

I would say that the Foo Fighters are the band I most associate with my recent medical issues and the force that has been the most there for me through this whole thing. Them and Taylor Hawkins and the Coattail Riders. I've been in a lot of pain for years now, but it has gotten steadily worse over time. In August of 2016, I rediscovered the Foo Fighters after years of being out of touch with their music. In September, my joint pain increased by ten fold. I basically hurt all over, all day, sometimes so much that I have trouble walking. The Foos gave me loads of great music to soothe my soul and my aching body and helped keep me sane while I tried to figure out what was wrong with me. I started watching videos on YouTube of interviews with the band that were hilarious and entertaining and helped distract me from how bad I felt all the time. Through these interviews, I learned about Taylor's side project Taylor Hawkins and the Coattail Riders, and started listening to them too. Those two albums remain some of the best rock music I've ever heard. Here, I had my arsenal to help me fight my way through the months to come.

In early 2017, I was finally able to see a doctor who ordered tests to try to make sense of my various symptoms. I waited for blood test results. I had the first CT scan of my life to see if I had a brain tumour or if there was something else going on in my head causing headaches and frequent bouts of vertigo. Those test results took three weeks. Have you ever had to wait three weeks to find out if you have a brain tumour or not? It's pretty nerve-racking. The Foos and the Coattail Riders got me through those three weeks. They made a great escape and comfort for me.

When the test results returned there was no brain tumour. Instead, I had cysts in my sinus cavities and a positive blood test for a tremendous amount of inflammation in my body. Add this to my other symptoms and it spelled out lupus as the diagnosis that made the most sense. I'm still in the middle of this. The rheumatologist I saw afterwards ordered more tests and said it's not lupus. After a year of trying to get used to the idea that I had a potentially fatal illness, I was back to square one with no diagnosis. This should have made me happy, that maybe it's not that serious, but in ways, it was just as upsetting, not knowing what to tell people when they ask me what's wrong. My Foos and my Coattail Riders are still helping me cope with what has been, and continues to be, a major ordeal.

Since then, my primary doctor has put me on medicine that helps with painful nerve disorders, thinking that since it isn't lupus, it could be something like fibromyalgia. And this medicine is working! I've been in far less pain since I started taking it. I still hurt, but the medicine has made such a tremendous difference. I still would like a diagnosis simply because it's my body and it would be nice to be able to put a name to what's happening to it, but as long as I have help, I can wait a bit longer. I've already been waiting this long!

During this process, I discovered that this nerve disorder is what causes me to have strange reactions to sound. Much of it is music-centred. I can't stand to hear rap or Tejano music played at a loud volume because the deep bass in those genres of music causes me great pain. For some reason, it just grinds into my nerves. The first time I heard the singing voice of Taylor Hawkins, I discovered that a sound could have the exact opposite effect on my body too.

There are unique qualities in his voice that soothe my hurt in a way no one else can. And trust me, I tested every singer in my music collection. It's something about the high, raspy quality of many of the notes he can hit. Those notes touch my nerves in a completely different way than the deep bass. It helps me with the pain, and it's quite profound to have a singing voice affect you this way, especially when you hurt as much as I was hurting. Because of this, Taylor will always be a very special person to me. I will always be thankful to him for sharing his beautiful, sexy singing voice with the world.

I don't know if people can really understand just how important a band can be until you've dealt with a health crisis and had people you've known for more than twenty years say absolutely nothing to you about it. You have a band that gives you song after song that soothes your soul and helps you deal with it every day, and they inevitably become extremely important to you. They say, "I'm sorry you're in pain. I hope this helps," with every note. I may cry during the concert in Dallas in 2018, but I'm sure I'll do my best to dance through most of it too.

Their sound is hard rock with the occasional heavy metal, punk, and/or pop touch. *These Days*, *Bridge Burning*, and *Times Like These* are some of my favourites that define the Foo Fighters sound for me, and they're the ones that I would tell someone to listen to if they wanted to hear what the band sounded like.

Most of my family and friends don't say much of anything when it comes to my love of the band. A few friends are very supportive to the point that they link me to any new articles or pictures that come up, including funny things like the cartoon of the Spice Girls with Dave's head that is captioned "Spice Grohls." Other friends talk to me quite often about how we feel about the band and its members, funny stories about them, band gossip, and the medical stuff I go through every day. There aren't many of these kinds of close friends, and I'm very thankful I found them so I don't have to be so alone.

I do talk about the band a lot on my journal and

Facebook. Most friends ignore it because they don't feel the same way about the band as I do or they don't understand why they mean so much to me. I've had friends say the Foo Fighters are mediocre or Taylor isn't attractive enough to warrant such a big reaction from me. They haven't experienced what I've experienced and they can't hear what I hear. Who knows why anyone hears an obsession when they listen to a particular band and someone else listening to the same song hears nothing of interest. It's a mystery process. All I know is I saw an amazing group of musicians who spoke to my soul at a time when I really needed them, and continue to do so.

Other friends simply understand and accept my love of these guys and link me to new songs and videos whenever they come across them.

There are a few friends who are also fans who are very supportive and talk about the band and its members with me all the time. I feel a special connection with them that I simply can't have with other people. They understand how a band and its music can help you make your way through life, especially when things get tough. This band can really bring people together.

Foo Fighters seem to be one of the last great hard rock bands of their generation. There aren't any new bands I can think of who will take over for them when they're forced to retire. The Foos are a holdover from the late 20th century who still rock as hard as bands half their age, and I hope that's how they will be remembered, and that kids will still be listening to them long after they're gone.

# Scott
## Ipswich, UK

Back in the last part of high school I got into different, alternative music, and was a big Iron Maiden fan, Queen, all that sort of stuff. Then it was purely by chance that a mate of mine said, "Oh, have you heard *Nevermind*?". And I was like, "What?". I'd just passed my driving test as well so one day I got an old cassette, chucked it in the player, and I'm driving along and I think it was either *Smells Like Teen Spirit* or *In Bloom* came on and I was like, "Oh. I like this. I like this a lot.". For probably about three or four months it was the only thing that was played in my car. Because I listened to that, I started looking a bit further back and had a look at *Bleach* and that was it. That was my love of the genre starting to build. We all know what happened to Kurt and I remember thinking, "Okay, maybe that's it.".

I always kept an eye on the music press. I used to be a big NME fan and one day I saw that Mr Grohl had been playing around in the studio. I thought, "Oh, perhaps he's going to bring out some new stuff. Perhaps he's going to go solo.". And then Foo Fighters self titled album came out and that was it. That's where my love began. Simple and straight forward as that! *Wattershed*, *Exhausted*, I just love them. Just absolutely love them.

It was literally a case of this was it; my music taste

was changing and this genre was becoming my main stay. Pearl Jam, etc. I even got in to Bush. I didn't get to see the Foo Fighters until probably when *One By One* came out. So I'd gone through the self titled calm, *The Colour and The Shape* etc and then *One By One* came out and that was the beginning of the gig season for me. My best friend worked for a company called InBev; they're the makers of Budweiser, Stella and stuff. And one day he phones me up and he says, "Scott, I've got a couple of production tickets to go to V [Festival]. Do you fancy coming with me?". And I'm like, "Oh yeah, I'm quite happy to do that. I've always wanted to go to V.". The night we went was the night that the Foos were playing just before Coldplay. So this was 2007 and we were there and just wandering around. We got in two hours early because we were production and just doing our thing. The evening wore on and I remember standing there in the crowd, we were probably a dozen rows back, and the intro of *All My Life* started and that was it. I went berserk! I was bouncing around in the crowd like some bloody lunatic and it was like I was fifteen all over again. They played the set and most of the songs were off *One By One*. I remember driving home and that night, Chris, my best mate at the time, said, "If you like them, you'll like these, too.". And he put Queens of the Stone Age on the car stereo. That was it; another band to add to the stable. And he said, "You know Dave Grohl drums on *Songs For The Deaf*?". I was like,

"Oh, I didn't realise that.".

I've always been in to music but I had this hiatus when I got married where I listened to it as and when I could. So their new album, *One By One,* was in the car, and once again, it was played to death. Then, on a personal level, things started turning bad because me and my ex-wife started going through a real tough patch. Believe it or not, *In Your Honor* came out and once again I was loving the new album. But *Stranger Things Have Happened* started becoming a bit of an anthem. She's a nurse in A&E and she'd been going out with all her mates from A&E and stuff like that. Me being dim, as I refer back to it now, wasn't seeing the signs of things going wrong. I started listening to *Stranger Things Have Happened* and it just seemed to sum up my life at that point. It was like I was sitting in bed, having my last smoke, and waiting for you to walk through the door. One line after another after another and it was just making such a connection. January 2009 was the dreaded morning. I'd not been at work that day because I'd been ill and she'd done a night shift and woke up and said that we needed to talk. And that was when the inevitable happened and she said that she wanted a separation. I lost it. I got in the car and I actually put *The Colour and The Shape* on. I remember *Big Me* coming on and I don't know why but that somehow calmed me down from going out and possible ragging the arse off the car and having an accident. So I went up to the cliffs just out of

Ipswich, up near Felixstowe. I had the windows open and the music on and I was sitting on my bonnet just listening to everything that was playing. I just thought, "Okay, I've got to make a life now.". It didn't come easy at all and it went to the point where I moved out of the family home. All the time the music was keeping me going.

I hit rock bottom and, this is the horrible side of everything that happened, one night I was in my best mate's house where I'd rented a room from him. I'd gone through a whole load of drink and a whole load of pills and I'm just laying on the bed thinking, "Okay, I'm feeling tired. Let's put some music on.". I'm lying there and, this is one of those I can "Come out of my body and see the whole scene as a film set" type moments. I put *One By One* on because it's always been my favourite album. Don't know why but it just has that connection with me. I'm lying there and *Times Like These* came on. And I just remember seeing the picture of my kids. As I looked at the kids, the line, "I'm a brand new sky to hang the stars upon tonight." came on. That was like someone poking me in the eye with a couple of matchsticks. It was at that moment that everything started to change. I did everything I could to make myself sick. I got myself up to Ipswich A&E and got my stomach pumped. All the time the song was rotating constantly in my head and the lyrics were hitting me hard. One of the things that I've always said that if I ever met Dave Grohl he would seriously have me on my knees, thanking him. Because if it wasn't for that song, if it hadn't been for those lyrics that had been written, I wouldn't be here. There's no two ways about it; I'd be dead. We all say that music saves our lives and sometimes I don't think the artists realise just how much impact their music has on us.

So a few weeks passed and it was a case of, "Okay, here we go. Let's start rebuilding.". And that flicks to song number two for me, my life post-marriage song. That's the way I look at it. There's pre-marriage, which was my last life, and now my new life. And it was *Learn To Fly*. Because it was a case of my demons are my bipolar, my depression, my anxiety disorder, and the borderline personality disorder. So the four things which technically make me were my demons. Every now and again I'd say, "Go and tell the angels that this might take all night.". And people would look at me as though to say, "What the Hell are you on about? What do you mean?". And I'd say, "One day you'll find out.". For ages it was all about me rebuilding myself, me rebuilding the confidence in myself and telling myself, "You know what? I can take life on. I can do this.". At this point I'm living for my kids and that's all that's going on.

My ex decided that she was going to move and she offered me my house back which, in some ways, was a bitter-sweet pill. But it was the only way that I was going to get a place of my own again because the cost of living in Ipswich is extortionate. I got the house back in mid-August 2009 and I walk in to this bare shell of a building. The house had been decimated and there was nothing left. I was like, "Wahey! I've got a blank canvas to work with.". So Foo Fighters posters started going up on the walls. It was like I was eighteen all over again! I even had a shrine to Grohl in the front room! Every time I came home from work, I'd whack on the music and it would either be a Foo track, or a Pearl Jam track, or Queens of the Stone Age. Whatever took my fancy at the time. One night, after going out on the lash, a whole load of us came back to the house and it was Tenacious D's *Pick of Destiny* and it was one of the funniest nights of my life. We were all sitting around until two or three in the morning, talking crap, and singing *Wonderboy* at the top of our lungs!

At that time I decided to change everything in my life. I quit my job as an insurance engineer and took on a massive role for me which was my first managerial role, running a car repair centre. I worked with a couple of other guys who were quite in to the Foos music and I made converts of some of the others. I always had music on in my office and, nine times out of ten, it would be the Foo. That's then where my angel comes in. It only took two years to find her! This particular day, Kerry, who was my wife's best friend came in because we'd just lost our receptionist and said, "Do you want someone to replace Dan?".

And I said, "Yeah, if you know of anyone, let me know.". Kerry told me that a friend of hers had just moved back from Wales. She'd had a horrible time and was looking to get in to some work. I told Kerry to bring her in and we'd have a chat and see how things went from there. So I met Lorna; she was brilliant, seemed right for the role, very fiery and would take no shit off of insurance companies. One night we all decided to go out for a pub quiz and make it a bit of a team bonding session. Anyone from work who wanted to come could. So me and her started chatting and the first thing that we had in common... Music. She loved anything different, loved her live music. She was a student and she'd come from a uni background and was ten years younger than me so it made me feel like I'd missed out!

We came back to Ipswich and decided to go for a drink at Issacs, which is on our waterfront and is a really nice place. Unfortunately, it was closing early so we decided to go for a wander up the quay. All the way along this walk, which was probably ten or fifteen minutes, we're swapping song lyrics. I'm hitting her with Foo Fighters lyrics and she's coming back to me with them. I was like, "Okay, this is spooky.". One thing lead to another and we started seeing each other. She put in a very, very big chase for me. I had to work my nuts off to get her! After six weeks, I finally end up with this beautiful lady.

So we start seeing each other and one night we're

sitting here, at home, and we'd just booked tickets to go and see the Goo Goo Dolls at UEA in Norwich. We're talking Foo Fighters and music in general and I said, "You know what? Foo Fighters have got a new album coming out called *Wasting Light* and they're going on tour.". Lorna said, "Really?!", and I said, "Yeah. Do you fancy going to see 'em?". And on an impulse, I was straight on to Ticketmaster, and ordered two tickets.

We end up going to Milton Keynes together [2011] and I'm not joking, next to my wedding to Lorna, it was one of the best days of my life. We went for the Sunday so we had John Paul Jones and Seasick Steve and it was brilliant, blindingly amazing. However, there was no bad side to it but there was a lot of tears because all the way up there, while we'd been driving along, *Walk* had come on the car stereo. Now *Walk* has more symbolisation for me now considering what happened last year than I'd ever imagine it would ever have [Scott went through a life saving knee operation in 2016]. But, back in 2011, it had a different meaning to me. In particular, the lyric "A millions miles away, your signal in the distance" really hit home because Lorna was in Wales and I was in Ipswich; how did it happen? How did we get pulled together? While we were listening to the song, the conversation turned to how we met, how we learned to love again, how we learned to talk and communicate, how there was that incredible connection between us, and how the song somehow connected us. That song brought us through a lot and every time we'd had an argument or anything like that, that would be the song that'd I'd play. Whether I'd been in the wrong or whether she'd been in the wrong or if life was just getting on top of us, *Walk* was the song that I'd go and listen to.

You fast forward, so to speak, because we had a quiet time when the tour was over and the music had disappeared.

And then we had Invictus [Foo Fighters played the closing ceremony of the first Invictus Games in London in 2014. Scott was involved in a campaign that helped to get a young carer to meet the band before the Invictus show.] .

What can we say about Invictus, I wonder?! I never ever, in a million years, thought that I'd get involved with what we got involved in. I got to meet Tom [from Given to Live, the organisation that helped to arrange the meeting with the band] and have a chat with him and, from that point forward, the band took on another meaning to me. They were no longer these rock gods. They were no longer these rock icons that I aspire to and who kept me going. They're now the same for other people, too. Music is one of those things that, in a way, is very self centred. We lose ourselves in our music and don't realise that the people we look up to are also the same people that others look up to as well. This was when I got on to the Foo Family page.

So me and Tom were talking that night and I asked whether he'd do a Twitter campaign. I think we spent seven or eight hours on the phone, most of the time with me being at work. And we began the tweeting, or "The Tweet Off" as I ended up calling it. Everyone used to take the mick out of me. They'd call me up and say, "Let us know when you're going on a massive Tweet-a-thon because we'll turn our phones off of vibrate"! It was like, "Wow! I'm tweeting directly to the band and to the management.". I remember spending one afternoon on the computer trying to get hold of Brendan, the band's old PA guy. I spent hours and hours and hours searching for information. Then a friend of mine pinged up on Facebook and said, "I don't know if this is going to help but I've got an old telephone number and an old address of where they [the old PA company] used to be in Hammersmith.". I don't think anything ever came of that information but the whole campaign was like everyone coming together with the common goal of getting Kayleigh to meet the band backstage. But also it was just like this wow factor of how the Foos music was getting a lot of people through a lot of hard times. Once again, my love for them became even bigger.

So we had Invictus and we managed to get Kayleigh to meet the band. That night was an amazing night for personal reasons as well and that was because of Phoebe, my middle daughter. Phoebe had gone through a massive episode of being bullied at school. She'd lost four stone in about six months and gone from this healthy, happy child to to this poor kid who didn't know her arse from her elbow. She felt useless and didn't want to exist any more. As Invictus came up I didn't think I stood a chance in Hell of going but I entered a competition through Vemo. They wanted you to send in why you loved Invictus. I also remember going on Kerrang and sending in an entry on there, too. I was at work on the Wednesday prior to Invictus and I'd just gone to the supermarket to grab something, which is how clearly I remember all of this. As I was waiting at the checkout, I was flicking through my emails and I saw this email from this girl called Kelly Smith. She was the organiser of the whole competition and it must have been a joint thing between Kerrang and Vemo. She'd sent me an email which said, "Congratulations, Scott, you've won two tickets to the Invictus Games closing ceremony.". I cried. I was walking along Colchester High Street crying because not only had I had the stuff with Tom going on but I'd also had a friend who were going through a bad time and I'd helped her to source tickets for the show. And now I was going to Invictus, too. All of it got on top of me at that moment.

I got home and said to Lorna, "Look, I've won two tickets to go to the Invictus closing ceremony. What shall I do?". She said, "Why don't you take Phoebe? Because Phoebe loves the Foos just as much as you do." So I phoned Phoebe and asked her if she wanted to go to a gig at the weekend. She said that she was a little bit nervous about it all. So I rephrased it and asked her if she wanted to go and see the Foo Fighters at the weekend... and the phone went dead! There were screams, there were screeches, and there were squeals!

The morning of the gig was fantastic because the hype on all the Facebook pages. I was talking with God knows how many people, people I'd never met, and they were becoming like friends overnight. Conversations were going on until stupid o'clock in the morning. I offered to help one of the girls who lived in Whitham to get to the venue, so I picked her up on the way down to the show. We parked at Hornchurch and caught the Tube to Stratford. I was all regaliaed up with my Foo Fighters tshirt and stuff like that. When we got down there, I remember waiting in the car park area because I'd said that I'd meet up with a couple of guys. And all these people were looking at me as they walked past me and saying Hi as they went. I remember thinking that I didn't have a clue who any of them were. Then the faces started to twig in my brain and I realised that it was the people that I'd been speaking to via the Foo fan pages.

There was one lady, Heidi from Ireland, who came

running over and gave me a huge hug. And that was it. So we went in to the venue [Queen Elizabeth Olympic Park, London] and I'm standing there talking to a group of them who were sitting in front of one of the speaker stacks. The next thing I knew I was accosted by Julie, who came flying over to me, bounded on my back, and screamed, "Scotty! How you doing?!". Then I bumped in to Gemma, who's become one of our family friends, as well as Dolgun and his misses, who live in Bedford. My in-laws live up that way so whenever we go and visit, we drop in and see them as well. And this network was building and building from this gig.

So we get our place in the pit and the opening bands came on. Then Prince Harry came on and he's doing his bit and we're all laughing and chanting. Finally, BOOM! Off it goes! I remember not looking at the stage but at Phoebe's face. At the time she was this little fourteen year old who's really life battered and weary already. All of a sudden, everything just melted away and there was this big grin from ear to ear because she was standing there seeing what her Dad saw eighteen years prior. In that moment, her love of the band was building and building and building. I remember them doing *The Pretender* and dropping in the riff from *Outside* [which was featured on 2014's *Sonic Highways*]. I looked at Phoebe and said, "That's new. There's some new material coming out!". And she was like, "Yeah, whatever, Dad. They're just playing around.".

There was a bit where we were both standing there and *Times Like These* came on and I bawled my eyes out. They played *Learn To Fly* and we're singing at the top of our lungs and bouncing around. Then, the one that got me the most that night because of how Phoebe reacted to it, was *Best Of You*. I just remember the tears, the crying, the hugging and, for her, that seemed to be an awakening because, ever since that show, that's been one of her anthems. Since then she's taken on life so strongly. It was the "Were you born to resist or be abused?" line that's really spurred her on and she's now taking everything in her stride. She's kicked the bullying up the arse and she's fighting whatever life throws at her. She's on anti-depressants, the same as her Dad, but she's a fighter. She got herself through school and she's now onto doing her A-levels at college. She's talking about going to university and, at the time, prior to that, she didn't have an aspirations. It was like the song and everything that it stood for gave her that impetus and, every now and again, we'll sit here and talk. One of the things that the band have bought about is that she now says that she and I have a  closer relationship because of them. We sit and talk music and, because of that, she feels like she can express herself more.

I remember walking out of the stadium after the Invictus show and everyone doing what I love, because they did it at Milton Keynes the first time I saw the Foo, and it was the "Woahs" from *Best Of You*. I remember going in to Stratford Tube Station and all you could hear was this chorus of the "Woahs". Me and Phoebe are walking along, belting it out as loud as we can. Got on the Tube, got to the car, had a drink, tried talking, and found that both of us had lost our voices!

Then we fast forward to the *Sonic Highways* period. Every Sunday, religiously, it was pray silence for the Foo Fighters in our house. What an immense piece of work that was. As soon as it came out on DVD, that was it, I'd got it. One night, me and Lorna were talking about all the different music we love. Once again, it was one of our music conversations that went on until three in the morning. She said, "What is it about the Foos that just captivates you?". I told her that it's because they're real. There's no pretence with them. Because you've got a bloke who could have just thrown it all away when Kurt died. Instead he took the bull by the horns and decided to make something out of what he'd got and that's been an inspiration to me from day one. Because I left school with nothing. My terminology is that I've always been stupid and everyone told me that I wasn't. But that's how I felt. I'd always pushed and pushed myself because I'd seen what Dave had done. And I got to the point where I ended up managing my own body shop. I had a huge team of people around me and I was looking after hundreds of thousands of pounds worth of cars. I always put it down to the fact that if Dave can do it musically then I can do it secularly. And I do. I don't give up because, at the end of the day, it's very easy to quit and call time. I've been there and I've almost done it and I'm glad that I didn't give up. And I owe that to the Foo Fighters through the songs and their dedication.

Lorna looked at me and said, "That's really amazing because, at the end of the day, you had something to latch on to and you latched on to the right thing. Whereas some people will latch on to drink or drugs to help them cope, you just latched on to music.". Music was, and still is, my drug. If there's a new album coming out I'm getting myself ready and getting it ordered so that I've got it ready to go on the day it comes out. It's been a case that there's been so many friendships made through music, and especially this band. This is where the *Sonic Highways* stuff really starts to peel in because when they announced the tour for Sunderland me and Lorna were broke. There was no way that we were going to get to any gigs. The friendships that I'd made and the way I'd helped people in the past was like a pay it forward coming in. I remember one night after everyone had bought the tickets and everyone's talking about Sunderland, Manchester, and Wembley. And I was sitting there thinking, "Wow. Wow. Wow. I wish, wish, wish I was going." when I got a phone call from Julie saying that my birthday was in May and that because I'd been such a support to her when she'd been going through some rough times she wanted me to go to Sunderland with her. I spoke to Lorna and she was fine with me going.

So 25th May [2015] there I was, rocking out in the pit. I was there, in the same venue, where I'd been to my first gig with Lorna and my first gig by myself where I knew only two other people. And now I was at a gig with twenty or thirty others that I know in the here and now. But now it's in a crowd of twenty thousand and I could safely say that I knew two hundred of the people in there through conversing on Facebook or text message. It was like, once again, how does a band do that? How does a band gel people together like that? Because we all come from different walks of life and different backgrounds. But when you put the music in there, and the Foos music especially, it knits us and we become like a community. And it is what it is; it is a community, a team, a lifestyle.

A couple of weeks later I get a phone call off of a guy who is now like a brother to me, Geoff. He said, "You're coming to Wembley, boy.". And I was thinking, *Shit! How do I tell Lorna that I'm going to Wembley as well?!* But it all panned out and I was allowed to go.

But things transpired, Dave broke his leg, and we were all absolutely devastated. However, we don't need Dave sometimes. We just get Jay and the boys involved [Foo Fighters tribute band – UK Foo Fighters]. There were some fundraiser gigs happening at a venue right next to Wembley Stadium and rather than let those gigs go to waste and cancel them, the UK Foos came and headlined for two nights. Oh man, I won't forget that night in a hurry! It was an immense, immense time and, once again, people were coming from all over the world. I remember talking to people and we were all chatting for months afterwards. It made me realise that these people, the Foo fans, are more friends than some of the people that I've known since school. We all take an interest and look out for each other. Once again, it's the connection with the music and the band.

When the Wembley gig didn't come off but they announced Milton Keynes, Geoff was straight on the phone to tell me that I was going to Milton Keynes. He'd told me that he was getting me a ticket to see the Foos and that if we weren't going to see them at Wembley then we'd damn well see them at Milton Keynes. Without hesitation I said yes. Although it was a little bit of a hard one to get round Lorna as I'd already been to two gigs, even if one of them was cancelled! I made it up to her by proposing at The Script concert.

So I went off to Milton Keynes. And then the wedding planning started. From the very beginning, we'd said that we were going to have a rock themed wedding. The first dance – now this was the hard bit –

was the one that we'd both had ideas about but which we both settled on the same song at the same point. And it was *Walk*. It was *the* song that we wanted. In between times, hospital happened and we all know what happened with me going in to hospital. I found out, through hospital notes that I'd been given and having spoken to my doctor, that if I hadn't gone in when I did  and had my first operation within two hours of hitting the hospital floor that I'd have lost my leg or I'd have been dead. So I didn't quite realise how serious it was. But all the time that I was in hospital, I had my Fighters (as I call them) all over the place. During that time, *Walk* took on that whole new meaning because it was literally a case of that I had to learn to walk again in the physical, as well as the mental, sense.

We got the hospital out of the way and I was going to get my suit sorted for the wedding. I went in to a suit shop in Ipswich to have one made. Lorna had said to me that she wanted me to wear something special, something that would make me feel like a million dollars on the day. We've gone in to this suit shop and we're talking to the guy and he asked me what I wanted. I said that I did and he pulled this liner out that was black with a skull motif. So I have a suit, that is a lovely shiny teal colour with this jet black lining with these skulls on it. While we were talking, he told me that he could do a bit of embroidery on the inside of the pocket as a little keepsake, like "To the one I love", or something like that. He said that I could have up to sixteen characters.

So me and Lorna sat down one night and went through every possible Foo Fighters title, working out how many letters are in them. Finally we'd got a list of the ones that had got the sixteen characters and one of them was "Learning to walk again 2016". She left it up to me to make the final decision so I went back down to the shop for the final bits and the guy asked me what I wanted doing. And I said, nice and simple, *No Way Back*. The guy was like, "What?! What does that mean?". I told him that, one, it was an absolutely epic tune by the Foo Fighters, and two, I'm walking down the aisle and there's no way back and that I didn't want to go back. The life that I have now, the one that I have with Lorna, is the best life that I could possible have. It's not always great, it's not always easy, but I don't want to go back to what I used to have. So that's now emblazoned on the inside lapel of my suit.

On the night of the wedding, we had everything playing, all of our favourite music, Biffy Clyro, Fallout Boy. You name it, we had it. The DJs we had were instructed that I wanted three songs. I wanted *Times Like These*, *Learn To Fly*, and then, to finish it, *No Way Back*. But then, we had the first dance and they did us a mash up of three songs that we wanted. This mash up starts off with *Hand On My Heart* by Olly Murrs, which goes into *Let Love In* by the Goo Goo Dolls, which then goes through in to *Walk*. It's mixed so well that it still makes the hairs on the backs of my arms stand up whenever I listen to it. The Olly Murrs song was ours. Then the DJs instructed people to come up on to the dance floor, which they did, and we had everyone dancing to *Let Love In*. When it went to *Walk*, I had Gemma, Geoff, Angie and Kev with us and I think that this Tudor building that we had the reception in nearly broke because we were all bouncing and singing! It got to the point that, after that night, I couldn't walk properly for two weeks afterwards!

That brings us up to the present day and I've got some bloody amazing memories that I've collected along the way. Because, when the Foos were due to play Hyde Park in 2007, they did three warm up gigs. One of them, and not many people know this, was in Ipswich. They played the Ipswich Regent. The set that they played for these little, random shows was the *Skin and Bones* set. I found out about this show and I camped from three in the morning, outside the Ipswich Regent, in the pissing rain, freezing my nuts off with my ex-wife giving me a lot of earache because she couldn't understand why I was doing it. But I got tickets and I got the front row. Granted we're sitting in a boring auditorium where you can't really get up and dance. But at the Ipswich Regent there's a gap of about eight feet between the seats and the edge of the stage. Of course I fucking danced! I made the most of it and I love it because there's not many people that was actually at that gig. I put something on one of the Facebook groups and I think it was Anne-Marie commented and said that she was there, at the Ipswich show. So there was someone there who I can say that I now know!

Then we jump forward again to the second time that I saw the Foos, which would have been V Festival. *In Your Honor* had just been released and the Foos were headlining V, which would have been 2007. At one point, we were walking across the field to see another band play when we wandered past the Channel 4 stage and see that there's a band called 606 playing. I wonder who 606 could be?! So I'm standing there, watching Dave Grohl and the boys doing a lot of the songs acoustically, and he does one of my top five Foos songs which was *But, Honestly*. So I saw it live then, and to fast forward to when I last saw them at Sunderland, and he did it there, too. And it completely blew me away because it sounded as good in 2015 as it did in 2007. I remember standing at Sunderland, crying, because I just love that song. Whenever I hear their songs, there's always emotions attached to them. It's one of those things; you can't put your finger on it totally, but I think it harkens back to how real the band members and songs are. How genuine, I think is the word I'd use, a band they are. They're not this KISS, or this Aerosmith, style. These guys are a bunch of blokes and, if you look at it, in some ways, come together ragtags who Dave has hand picked because he sees how good they are and sees what they are as a team. And you put that together and, my God, that is a mighty force. That is an amazing sound. They go off and do their own things and they always come back together. And we all cry when they say that they're having a bit of a break. And we're always the first ones waiting for the announcements and new albums. Because they, in some ways, are like life blood to us and I think that will always be that way. When I'm eighty five years old, I will still be walking down the road, looking at my arm where I've got my *Times Like These* tattoo because I'll always think, "Them boys saved my life.". My little one, Alana, now regularly asks me, "Daddy. Put concert on. Put music on.". She loves the Wembley gig and she runs around here like an absolute fruit-loop when it's on! When they did the Cheese and Grain I thought that I'd try and get her to bed and then I could have the TV on or watch it on You Tube. She came down from bed and wouldn't move from the sofa. She wanted to watch the whole gig! She was bouncing around and loving it. I've got three kids, four soon because Lorna's pregnant, and all three of my girls, in some way, love the Foos. Phoebe definitely does and Chloe has her Foo Fighters songs that remind her of her Dad. I know it sounds morbid but when I'm dead and buried if one of those songs come on it's going to be nice to know that they're going to remember their Dad because of that song, because of the boys, because of the band.

The Foos are just something special. For all the slating that they sometimes get and, "Oh, Dave's the nicest man in rock" and all of that, so what? You know what, he may be. But, at the end of the day, he's just a human being. But he's a human being that's got an amazing talent. He connects with people and I think that's what a lot of the music press and suchlike don't like because he is that type of person. And the press think that there's got to be some shit on him and that he can't be that nice all the time. Well, maybe he's not but, at the end of the day, he's human and he *connects*. And I think that's what the whole ethos of Foo Fighters is; connection with the fans. Every time, at the end of a gig, they say, "Thanks guys. You give us the best job in the world.". I think that's what makes them and I think that's why so many of us connect to them in one way or another. It's like, the friends that I've made is through that common interest in the band and the way that we all come together because of them. I think that's what I love about it all.

In fifty years time, I think they're going to be one of those bands that people are going to look back on and say, "They may not have been a genre defining band but they kept something going that was dying. They kept rock music going." Because they have. They've kept the whole stage show and ambience of the genre alive. Dave, with everything that he does for the industry as a whole such as *Sound City* and *Sonic Highways* and the way that he says what he thinks, like he did at South By South West, is just so inspiring. He inspires people to do what they want to do in life. I'd like to think that, in fifty years time, that some people will look back and know that they're playing music because they were inspired by the Foo Fighters and because they listened to what Dave had to say. The Foos are no Beatles. They're no revolutionaries, so to speak, of the genre. But they are, as we've said so many times before, real live rock music.

Unfortunately, that's what's dying and I hope that they keep on turning out album after album for the next twenty years. I think that their music will live on, even when the band is gone, because of the whole ethos around the band, the ethos of connecting to and bringing people together. I think their legacy will be that. It'll be the realness, the lack of pretension, and the wanting to experiment and keep on bringing new stuff to the table as well as inspiring others and showing that things can be done in the face of adversity. Not many people these days will experiment. The Foos did with *Wasting Light* and with *Sonic Highways*. I think that's the kind of things that people will remember. They'll remember the band that played in a garage [Foo Fighters did a tour of fans garages in 2011] or the secret warm up shows they did for Invictus Games when they played in tiny venues as The Holy Shits. The Garage Tour? Can you imagine someone like U2 doing that? It wouldn't happen! I'd like to think that those are the kinds of things that the Foos will leave behind and that the people in fifty years time, and well in to the future, will come across.

Dave, Taylor, Nate, Chris, Pat: If you ever read this, I love you guys! And thank you so much!

# AFTERWORD

The stadium is packed with sixty thousand people. An unseen electricity ripples through the night air, tickling the back of your neck and making you shiver. Several months ago, you went in to battle with thousands of others to buy a ticket for this event and the expectations have been riding high ever since.

You're pressed against the cold steel of the rail that separates you from the front of the stage. Your eyes are trained on the mostly darkened stage. Just a single light is lit, illuminating the logo that hangs amid the darkness. Around you, the tense excitement rises another notch as the magical hour draws ever closer. The weight of thousands of other people presses closely against your back, their emotions running as high as yours are. Like you, they've waited months for this moment. In your mind you can hear, see, and feel every moment that lies before you.

The first notes of music ring through the air and the weeks of waiting snap like a tree branch. People scream and cheer as the band finally steps onto the stage. You let go of the rail, unaware that your knuckles have turned white from how tightly you've been holding it, and you lift your arms above your head. Your voice rings out with the thousands of others and you open your hands as though to try and capture the music, the moment, the energy, and hold on to it forever. The first song thunders over the packed stadium and every person joins in, their voices becoming one.

Being a music fan can mean many different things to many different people. For some people, they may keep their love of a band to themselves. They go about their days, maybe collecting albums and only coming out when a tour is announced.

For others, being a fan is full time commitment. Between the chores of their day to day lives, they proclaim their love for a band far and wide. They collect everything that their favourite musicians put out and avidly follow any side projects. Their chosen band inspire them to create artwork, music, and many other things. They form close knit groups with other fans and create places, often online, that give them a space to share their love. For them, the band is their church and they, the fans, are the congregation.

I'll admit it; I'm not the world's biggest Foo Fighters fan. There's, at most, five or six songs that I'll listen to on a regular basis. But I'm not much for rocky-pop ballads. They just don't float my boat. Sorry. I'm more likely to be at a heavy metal concert. It makes people laugh that I'm writing a book about Foo Fighters and their fans. But there's a reason for that.

What really pulled me in to the band's orbit was their enthusiasm and their love for music. They're willing to share a stage with pretty much anyone and give time to the smallest and newest of bands. They have time for their fans, posing for photographs and making dreams come true. The stories of their love, kindness, and humility abound on the internet. They are, in essence, the perfect band, one that creates thundering, stadium filling rock songs while remaining humble and down to Earth enough to step up to a new musician and say, "Hi. I'd love to talk to you.".

My own story with the Foo Fighters, and their fans, began in 2013 when my path crossed those belonging to Julie and Kirri. We all met on a writing website and, while they were already friends, they decided that they'd like to get to know me, too. As huge fans of the Foos, they were determined to try and pique my interest. Happy in my own little musical bubble, I refused everything that they sent to me. That was until they discovered my Achille's Heel.

I don't care for much that's put out on to television but I do love documentaries. Give me a series, or a film, and I'll devour it in a single sitting. More often than not, I'll rewatch it to the point of obsession. At the same time as Julie and Kirri were nudging me towards the Foos, Dave Grohl's documentary about the Van Nuys studio Sound City had just been released. My friends saw it as a perfect way to ease me in to meeting Foo Fighters. They weren't wrong and *Sound City* is one of the most watched films in my collection. In early 2014, we visited the studio together (now known as Fairfax Recordings).

At the time, I thought that was the end and that my

two wonderful friends would let me idle through the fandom and come out the other side so that I could continue my love of other bands. But it wasn't going to end there.

In late 2014 UK fans organised a Kickstarter in an attempt to bring the band to Birmingham. Despite being in the heart of the country, Birmingham is often overlooked as a tour destination. It's also the city that I regularly visit to go and see bands play. The idea of bringing a bigger band to Birmingham was a brilliant idea and one that inspired me far more than I thought it would. So I started blogging about their Kickstarter and inadvertently found myself surrounded by Foo Fighters fans. My website stats went through the roof as they shared the posts and the social media response was overwhelming.

The rise of social media has given fans around the world a greater power to get in touch with one another. With everyone connected to their phones, tablets, and computers, people can now form the groups and bonds that they could only dream about when the Foo Fighters formed back in 1995. Social media has allowed people to create easy to manage forums and ways of tracking users. More often than not, Foo Fighters fans go under the name "Foo Family". At the time of writing, the largest group is hosted on Facebook and has nearly 15,000 members.

The Foo Family are a group of people who wear their hearts on their sleeves. Forever willing to help out anyone who's in distress, they regularly raise money for charity. Their members are wild, innovative spirits who create everything from t-shirts to posters to jewellery to music. They tour with one another, meeting up at Foo Fighters and tribute band shows. Their homes are open for whoever needs them, safe spaces away from a world that may otherwise shun them for their passion. They follow the band's side projects with a fervour that isn't seen among other groups of fans.

Passion. It's possibly the only word that can be used to describe Foo Fighters fans. It runs through their veins and is the energy that makes their heart beat.

It was their passion that, back in 2014, lead me to making the promise that I would one day write a book about them. I'd interview the fans and tell their stories before leaving them with the final product; a physical reminder of all that they are. Everything about their love for the Foo Fighters would be documented. The highs, the lows, the celebrations, the friendships, the relationships, and everything in between. Along the way, and thanks in part to the fans, I've fallen in love with the band and all that they do.

This is that book and these are their stories.

# WEBSITES

Pretty much everyone who's in this book has a website that's dedicated to, or inspired by, Foo Fighters. You can find them online at the following links.

You can find Ollie, and the UK Foo Fighters, at:
www.ukfoofighters.co.uk

Simon, Kirri, and Foo Fighters Live:
www.foofighterslive.com

Nik's band, From Day One:
www.fromdayone.net

Stefano and his documentary, Dreaming of Foo Fighters:
www.dreamingoffoofighters.com

John, and Fu Fighters, are at:
www.fufighters.co.uk

You can find the Fooz Fighters online at:

Website: www.foozfighters.com
Facebook: www.facebook.com/foozfightersband
Instagram: @foozfighters
Twitter: @foozfightersband


The UK Foo Family website, and their merchandise, can be found at:
www.FooFightersUK.com


Sarah, and her various pages, are at:

Taylor Hawkins Fan Page:
www.facebook.com/taylorhawkinsfanpage

Wiley Hodgden Fan Page:
www.facebook.com/wileyhodgdenfanpage

# ACKNOWLEDGEMENTS

Julie and Kirri, without who this journey would never have been taken. May there be many more adventures together in the future.

Sarah, aka the Puzzle Mistress. Thank you for the late night phone calls and early morning text messages as well as for being my guide during this project. Your love and support over the course of this book has meant so very much to me. May the good times roll!

Sue and Steve Marsh, because, without you, there would be no book. Thank you so much for nudging me to write this and for all your ongoing love. The world is a better place with you in it.

Kate, for being the person who helped me through a lot of the stress. Thank you for all the geeking out, for all the laughter, and for helping to piece this together.

The global Foo Family: Thank you for your love, patience, and for being so willing to share your stories with the world. Your strength and perseverance through life's storms say so much about you and I feel truly blessed to have been given the opportunity to share your lives with the world. All that you've done, and all that you're going to do, will never be forgotten.

Last, but not least, my own family without who there would be no music. Thank you for all that you do and for allowing us to follow our dreams, musical or otherwise. Your love for everyone who steps in to your lives is an inspiration and one that I aim to live by. May you be forever blessed with all that is good.

# ABOUT THE AUTHOR

Rachael currently lives just outside of Leicester, England and grew up in a house filled with music. When she's not writing, she enjoys travelling, reading, and UFOlogy. *Send in the Congregation* is her first non-fiction book.

www.raegee.co.uk
Instagram: @RoswellPublishing
Twitter: @VeetuIndustries
Facebook: facebook.com/thequeenofsteam

"No-one is you, and that is your power."
- Dave Grohl

11324081R00110

Made in the USA
Lexington, KY
09 October 2018